MAN ON FIRE

THE LIFE AND OTHER ACCIDENTS
OF JIM DOWDALL

STUNTMAN

MAN ON FIRE

THE LIFE AND OTHER ACCIDENTS OF JIM DOWDALL

STUNTMAN

JIM DOWDALL WITH GRAHAM SCOTT

THE MESSAGE MEDIUM

2019

Published by
My Memoirs & Me with The Message Medium

ISBN: 978-1-9999381-5-4

Disclaimer
I have tried to recreate events, locales and conversations from my memories of
them. Memory is fickle, and I freely acknowledge that others may remember
events differently. In order to maintain their anonymity in some instances I may
have changed the names of individuals and places, but I've tried to remember
events as they happened.

Our thanks to Andrew Illes for design and production.

To Bev and Jordan,

who suffered long and hard over the years.

They had to play second fiddle to 'tomorrow's chip paper'

that is so often the film business.

But, just occasionally, we did something memorable.

Contents

Foreword
by James May

Officially, I've known Jim Dowdall for 17 years, during which time he has often been responsible for safeguarding my well-being in times of great peril. Or at least while filming *Top Gear* and *The Grand Tour*. But soon after meeting him I discovered that I'd actually known him since I was six.

It was then, as an excitable boy, that I was taken by my father to see the newly released film *Battle of Britain*. Jim, a mere lad himself in 1968 and the only person on set who could operate the weapons convincingly, was the nose gunner in a Heinkel 111. I can still see him now. I think he gets his head shot off in that.

Later, in *Where Eagles Dare*, he is the German soldier behind the machine gun (that he could no doubt describe in excruciating detail) in that huge shoot-out in the schloss. I think he gets blown up by a grenade in that.

Much later, but still a good ten years before I met the real man, he was expertly cast as a witless and chubby-faced Wehrmacht trooper advancing on the surviving Jude Law in that first sniping scene in *Enemy at the Gates*. 'I bet he gets shot,' said my then-girlfriend. Spoiler alert: he does.

I'm sure I've unknowingly seen Jim many more times in countless other action, adventure, sci-fi, and war films. *Star Wars*, for example. I'm fairly confident he usually buys the farm.

It's an odd life, his, as you are about to read. He once ran away to the circus, which is not quite so surprising once you know him. He did a spell in the military, worked as an armourer, as a stunt man, and finally in the role where I now encounter him regularly, as a stunt co-ordinator. As a result of this his speech is a strange conflation of army shorthand, the script of a shelved 1950s war film, and idioms of his own making, such as: 'They don't know the difference between fish-fingers and Thursday'. I often use that one myself.

What makes it a pleasure to write this introduction is that the opportunity exists at all. I don't mean because Jim Dowdall has possibly saved me from drowning in the past, but because this man who has died so many times for our on-screen entertainment is very much still here. He worked in the film and TV business in an era when stunts were real, and stuntmen ensured the safety of the big stars while no-one worried enough about theirs. The darkest of Jim's anecdotes (there are many, and they're quite lengthy) are the ones about colleagues who didn't make it.

But here he is, at however many hundred years old he is, still regularly teetering at the top of a scaffolding, upside-down in a car, strapped to a zip-wire, or whatever. He really should give it up while he's ahead.

JAMES MAY

1

AIM HIGH

'The ladder of success is never crowded at the top.' Napoleon Hill

I often get asked what was the most memorable stunt that I've done. There are quite a few to choose from. I've been set on fire dozens of times; I've been knocked off a horse and dragged; been shot by an arrow; crashed and turned over more motorcycles and cars than I care to remember; fallen through toughened glass and jumped out of a second-storey window onto concrete – and had a wardrobe land on my head.

But the stunt that really springs to mind involved me standing at the top of a ladder. I didn't have to fall off it or anything, I just had to stand there, painting a wall.

It was for a commercial for the chocolate Yorkie Bar in the late 1980s and it started with a close-up of a decorator painting a white wall. That was me. Then the camera draws back and we see he's standing on a ladder, then we pull back further and we see he's standing at the very top of an enormously tall ladder and he's painting the White Cliffs of Dover.

I'm not wild about heights but the lure of the £50 notes overcomes a lot of one's nervousness. Back then, the technology wouldn't allow us to have a safety harness which could be digitally removed. There was no safety harness, no wire, just me about 140ft up a ladder with a sea wind gusting. It had been challenging enough just getting the ladder built.

It had been made in separate steel sections which then had to be bolted together. Each section was lowered from the top so the ladder was built from the ground up. And up. I was down there, with a safety line on, bolting the sections together as they came down, which involved gently pushing myself and the ladder away from the cliff so the next section could go on. Eventually I was about 140 or 150ft up in the air and the ladder was built.

"""

After being hauled to the top to change into a painter's overalls, I then abseiled down again, complete with paintbrush and bucket. Going backwards off the top of that cliff wasn't easy for me. Then I stood at the top of the ladder and the safety line was taken away. I clung on. Through the walkie-talkie I heard 'Action' and started 'painting' the cliffs as the helicopter out to sea got the shots.

The ladder had some flex in it, so it moved about a bit and the wind would gust in and shift it some more. Every time it moved my heart missed a beat. Like I say, I'm not much of a heights guy, but this job was a real challenge as I dislike giving in to nervousness, something which can be overcome with a bit of determination.

When it was done I did breathe a sigh of relief, but then remembered we had to dismantle the ladder so I had to do it all again in reverse. Then I breathed a slightly bigger sigh of relief.

But before the job even began I'd worked out the odds on the construction of the ladder, the wind speeds that day, whether it would be onshore or offshore, the integrity of my equipment and every other detail, so I felt as if I'd eliminated as many risks as possible. That's what stunt people do, since they're far more risk-averse than the average person in the street.

You assess the risks of what you're doing and work it out as a percentage and then charge based on that percentage. Then, if the risk percentage looks okay and you want to do the job and they agree the fee, you do the job. I was being paid a lot of money to stand on that ladder.

It was a similar job to one I'd done a few years earlier. I'd gone up for a commercial advertising milk for the Milk Marketing Board. The slogan was: 'Gotta Lotta Bottle!' There were two jobs going. The first was putting one's head into a lion's mouth and the second was a helicopter shot of a guy seemingly painting some metal girders which then pulls back to reveal that he's actually painting the Forth Bridge. Having worked in the circus with lions, I had no problem with the lion's mouth and hoped I'd get that one. Guess which one I got.

It was a sunny but very cold day in February and, having spent nearly an hour climbing up the girders and getting very hot, I prepared to take out the thermals I'd brought up with me in a backpack to change into. I knew I was going to be there for some hours. I was thrilled to find that one of the two milk bottles I was carrying in the pack had broken and all the thermals were soaked. I got very, very cold, and was so grateful to come back down after five hours up there.

You might well wonder why I was doing such things. But I was never going to be a solicitor or someone who was going to get a regular salary. Instead I'd found other ways to make a living, even if precisely none of them met with my mother's approval. Never getting her approval was tough, but she was having to do two parental jobs as my father (who was an alcoholic) had topped himself when I was quite young.

My parents' marriage certificate and my birth certificate differ by about eight weeks, so that tells a story on its own. It was my father's third marriage but, really, he was married to the Chelsea Potter pub in London's King's Road.

He'd been a barrister before World War II and a journalist during the war and, due to his upbringing, he'd always been a big drinker. I didn't really see a great deal of him because he'd either be at the pub or at his office, in a West London advertising agency. Barrister, journalist, ad agency – all big drinking industries back then.

My mother had a bit of a drinking problem too, but she had it more or less under control…ish! Things could be a bit chaotic but I was lucky. Bless her heart, my maternal grandmother picked up the bill for my education. That meant I went to a pre-prep school, Hill House, which was in Chelsea, just behind Harrods. I shared a bench with Prince Charles. As you do.

We used to go and play football at the Duke of York's Headquarters in the King's Road. I was a very athletic kid and one day I had the ball and was charging hard when I felt this really rough pull on my shoulder from behind. That was bang out of order. So I turned and hit the boy hard and then realised it was Prince Charles. I remember thinking 'I could go to the Tower for this'. Really. Unfortunately the paparazzi were outside the grounds and it was all over the papers. I wrote to him when he was about to get married (for the first time) and he sent me a nice hand-written note back, so I think I've got away with it.

After that I got sent to a minor public school near Eastbourne, and I arrived not long before sports day in the summer term. I won every single thing I competed in – except for the long jump, where I came third. I won the Victor Ludorum without really trying. I thought it was a piece of cake. I'd found something I was good at.

I started gymnastics and won junior, intermediate and senior cups and then won the Sussex gymnastics boys' cup. That was going so well, but the academic side was less than stellar shall we say. And then I was asked to leave that particular establishment.

I'd been doing some shooting at the school's .22 rifle range. At the end of one day I 'borrowed' a rifle and shot a fox. I had the hunting instinct. I might have got away with that but then I hung the fox up on the school flagpole. Someone ratted me out and I left for a daytime tutorial establishment in Holland Park.

It was a very expensive place, bless my grandmother again, and they really tried – just half a dozen of us to a class and so on – but they had no gymnastics, no football, no games, so there was no chance for me to shine at the things I was good at. I got one O-level, in English Language, and at 16 the school thought I ought to go off and do something more physical. So I joined the circus.

2

From the Circus to the Armoury

'Maybe I am a little bit of a clown, but I am also a serious sportsman.'
Eddie the Eagle

My parents and grandparents tried to give me an education that would allow me to get a 'proper job', but part of the reason I'd been sent to a boarding school was to get me out of the home environment.

My father was coming home drunk every single night. He wasn't a nasty drunk, he'd never hit my mother or anything. He was a laughing drunk, a nice drunk, but I could hear him falling over the furniture and my mother berating him. Like I say, she was borderline alcoholic too, but controlled it better.

Things changed when I was about nine or so. She'd kicked him out of the house a year earlier, so I hadn't seen much of him. Then my mother told me he'd accidentally taken a couple of pills when he was drunk and had died. I remember brushing it off at the time. But when I was in my early twenties I found out (from my half sister Kate, who was living on a houseboat in Sausalito, California) that he'd wanted to come back for Christmas, but my mother had said 'No' as he was such a disruptive influence. He'd then deliberately had a bath, and then took himself to bed with a bottle of whisky and some sleeping pills. I've always thought it was a very selfish gesture by him, because it's the people who are left behind who get completely screwed up.

My mother was very keen on telling the 16-year-old me that I was an oxygen thief so I always felt like I had to prove myself. My mother felt I needed to have got O-Levels and A-Levels and so only bad could befall me.

But one of the things I'd discovered at that posh Holland Park school was motorbikes, since some of the other boys there had them. After I'd left (following school reports about 'you can lead a horse to water') I washed cars and polished shoes and saved up £100, which allowed me to walk into Pride & Clarke – in the 1960s it was one of the largest motorcycle shops in the world. I bought a Honda 125 but soon swapped it for a BSA C15, a 250cc motorbike and the biggest you could ride on L-plates. My mother went absolutely spare.

But I had mobility, independence, and petrol was cheap. Unlike today, in those days there was a real stigma to being 'on the dole' (unemployed) and I was determined not to go there. One day I rode over to Ascot and asked Bertram Mills Circus if they had a job. They gave me a job on the spot, as a roustabout. Bertram Mills was famous for its Christmas show at Olympia and, by Christmas 1964, I was working with the lion trainer, Gerd Siemoneit. We roustabouts had to get the cage set up on the main stage during the interval, then get it taken down and away in about four minutes while he did his bows at the end of the act.

I was putting up chairs, cleaning out cages, and just occasionally standing in for a clown who wanted a day off. I'd be on the stage, walking on my hands, doing flic-flacs, tripping over, all that stuff, in front of a big audience every day. It was fun, but the period after Christmas isn't a busy one for a circus, so I was intrigued to be offered a job at a circus in Sweden that would have given me some welcome security.

I talked about it with some of the people I knew at the circus and they told me that it was like a big family. Some of them had been there for about 27 years. And I didn't feel like I had a proper family so I was really tempted. But I didn't want to be a roustabout in 27 years' time so I left, with no idea what to do next.

The jobs I did next horrified my mother, as I was sometimes living at home, still a teenager, although I always paid my own way. And they were object lessons in showing that nothing in life is wasted.

I did a few things, like working at Pride & Clarke, where I'd bought my first motorbike. I was breaking second-hand bikes down for spares, a filthy job but one that taught me how an engine worked, how pistons moved in the bores, what a camshaft did, so it was all hugely valuable for later.

It was a filthy job, and I'd come home grubby and oily every single night. Mum wouldn't let me sit down for dinner until I'd got cleaned up, although she hated the oily ring I'd leave round the bath every time.

This was in the 1960s, remember. We lived just off the King's Road in Chelsea in a tiny three-floored house in Bywater Street, and on Saturday afternoons I'd go and sit at the end of the cul-de-sac on my motorbike and watch the world go by. Those were Sergeant Pepper days, and you'd see people in the most amazing outfits who'd like to promenade past. The Rolling Stones, the Beatles, they all came, with red tunics, bell bottoms, platform shoes and long, long hair. It was all the most outrageous stuff for that time, and it was most entertaining to be in the epicentre surrounded by the Mary Quant and Granny Takes a Trip boutiques.

And there was me in Levi jeans, plaid shirt, black boots and a black leather jacket. I was a 'rocker' and was a member of the 59 Club (the rockers club) and went out looking for 'aggro' with 'mods'. Not long after I'd grown out of that, I swapped the boots for trainers and bought straight 501 jeans years before they became a really hot brand simply because they were comfortable and not flared. I hated 'fashion' as such – why would everyone try to look the same?

I moved on to washing cars at Kennings Car Hire. We had to drive the cars into the wash area and then park them in bays where you had about three inches of leeway either side, so you had to get out the window. These were cars like the Morris 1100, or you could go all the way up to a Morris Oxford if you were flash.

I didn't have a driving licence but the job was a great exercise in spatial awareness and how to park a car in really tight circumstances. If we caused any damage then we paid for it. You never know where things lead and those apparently mundane jobs helped my career as a stuntman, no question.

Mind you, my mother was horrified that I should be earning a living washing cars. This meant she was even more pissed off when a Christmas job at Harrods was cut short because I got caught smoking on the escalator. If you were a customer you could smoke a cigar on a tripod, but anyone wearing a staff pin, like me, was forbidden from smoking anything. Filthy habit anyway.

I was out of work again, but I was really getting into 20th Century military history, despite not having a History O-level. I would read anything on the subject, and this was about the time of the *Purnell's History of the Second World War*, a huge weekly part-work. I mentioned earlier that my father had been married twice before, and I had two half-sisters. One of them, Kate, got a job on the series as assistant picture editor.

Trouble was, she didn't know much about the subject. So I'd see a photo with a caption reading 'German artillery piece firing on the Eastern Front', and I'd go 'Well, that's an 88mm at Stalingrad isn't it?'. Turns out, in my opinion, neither Kate nor her picture editor knew much about military kit at all. And I did, so I'd end up doing a bit of work for them.

I loved guns and was always looking at *War Picture Library* publications because the artists back then were people who'd served during the war so they drew really accurate MG 34s or Stukas or whatever. And I learned a lot from those little magazines.

One of the places Kate went to research for photos was a firm called Bapty & Co, which did have a massive picture library, but its main business was as a theatrical supplier of military equipment, weapons and military vehicles. Kate had a word with the boss and told him her brother was mad about guns and needed a job. He gave me a job. I'd been earning £12 a week at Harrods and now I was an apprentice on £8 a week. But I would have paid to work at Bapty.

3

THE DIRTY DOZEN

'Just walk slow, act dumb and look stupid.'
Major Reisman (Lee Marvin), The Dirty Dozen

'Apprentice armourer'. That was my job title, and I loved the job. I was 18, working in a building that was four floors of swords, daggers and firearms from every period in history. I was taking guns apart, learning about them, cleaning them and putting them back together again. In the lunch hour, instead of eating a sandwich and picking my nose, I'd be in the picture library on the second floor, reading and reading about WWI, WWII, the Wild West, whatever. I just sucked it all up.

Back then nobody worried much about gun safety. We were handling real weapons that had been converted to fire blanks for films. For most weapons that just meant a restrictor in the barrel, and therefore the gases from the blank would recycle the weapon, whether it was gas fed or recoil fed. Take out the restrictor and you were back to a real firearm again – and I'm handling MP 38s, Bren guns, MG 34s, you name it.

I couldn't have been happier, but I hadn't been there long before they told me I was going to be assistant armourer on a film. I'd be cleaning the guns and looking after them and then handing them out to the actors while the chief armourer would be in the truck repairing the weapons and stuff. The film was to be called *The Dirty Dozen*.

Fast forward and I knock on a door. I've just been to see Donald Sutherland and shown him how the guns would work as filming got under way. He had been totally laid back, like his later character in *Kelly's Heroes*. Then I'd been to see one of my all-time heroes as a boy, Charlie Bronson. And he'd told me he knew how to fire a gun and I was to get lost. Big disappointment. Now I knock on another door.

I've got an M3 sub-machine gun over my shoulder and I go in. It's 10am and Lee Marvin is sitting there in a dressing gown with his feet up and a cigar and a bottle of Jack Daniels on the go. He invites me in and tells me to do my thing with the guns. So I start, telling him: 'This is a M3 "grease gun"' and going through the basics, like telling him the empties spill out the right hand side and they'll be hot and there's quite a muzzle blast and you have to be careful and so on.

And he's sitting there looking up at me and he reaches out and takes the gun and then engages me in conversation. Meanwhile he's stripping the gun down without breaking eye contact with me, then he puts the component parts on the desk. He stops talking for a minute and looks down and there's everything laid out in the approved order, then he looks up and start talking again and reassembles it without looking at it.

I'm aware this is going on but I'm trying to hold eye contact with him at the same time. Then he cocks it and hands it to me with the magazine empty in the approved military fashion, and I look at the gun and go 'Right'!

I walked out of the room with my tail between my legs, not realising that he had served in the Marine Corps during the war and had been wounded in action, on Saipan. He knew about this stuff for real. From then on our relationship was magnificent. I'd give him his gun in the morning and he'd carry it with him everywhere, then he'd ask for 'Jimmy' at lunchtime so he could hand it back to me, cocked and empty, and then after lunch, he'd take it for the afternoon and carefully hand it back to me at the end of the day.

He was a proper professional, and one of the great moments in my career came about 20 years later in 1985, when we were making *The Dirty Dozen: Next Mission*, which was a really bad made-for-television exploitation film. But Lee Marvin was there. He was dying from emphysema and it was almost his last film, which was a sad end. But I hadn't seen him between the two films and I was now a stunt performer and dressed as a German motorcycle rider with all the gear including the helmet on my head. I went into the dining bus with my breakfast and this man at the other end of the bus looked at me, and then made a gesture as if he was cocking a grease gun and showing me. Being recognised and acknowledged by Lee Marvin – that's a moment.

But on that first film I didn't get carried away. I was an 18-year-old rocker and I was cocky bollocks but I wasn't stupid. I was suddenly thrown in with all these big stars but I was respectful of their position, even when – like Bronson – they were rude to me. And we were busy.

Remember the chateau scene, where the Germans are trapped below ground? We shot during the day, but then we shot six weeks of nights. I was young, I thought I could work all day and all night forever, but you soon learn about your own robustness. After the third night I was hanging in rags but the whole shoot was about 14 weeks. That chateau episode kept all three armourers busy the whole time, mostly just reloading weapons.

It was a very sharp learning curve as you're working on a very expensive set with very famous actors and if a gun doesn't fire properly you have to have a spare instantly ready and then find out why the other one stopped. Guns aren't designed to fire blanks so you have to nurse them. The condition of the magazine is also critical, as it's a major cause of jams.

I discovered two 'grease guns' (as the M3 was known as in the US Army) that would work relatively faultlessly, and they became the Marvin and Bronson guns. I used to keep those guns with me and keep the magazines separate in my jacket or whatever so they'd always be ready to go. The whole situation wasn't helped by Bronson's habit of literally just throwing his gun down at lunchtime, so I'd have to anticipate him and be there, asking to take the gun from him.

Then it was time to blow the chateau up as one of the climactic scenes. And just before that happened, some kids got on the set and set fire to it, so they had to rebuild the chateau again – so we could blow it up.

◉◉◉

You remember the massive half-track at the chateau? That was one of Bapty's, and I was learning about vehicles too. At that time I had an Austin Champ as my daily transport in London. Yeah, a 3.0-litre military vehicle with four-wheel drive, driven in London by an 18-year-old who works in the film industry. Getting that insured was interesting.

Actually, it would probably be impossible for me to insure such a combination now if I was 18 again, but that was only the half of it. I was so involved with what I was doing that really all I thought about was guns and motorbikes and history. But I did have a sort-of girlfriend, and I'd go and pick her up after work in the Champ when I was in London. The Champ didn't have any doors or side curtains, and I'd have maybe 20 MP 40 sub-machine guns stacked in the back behind the seats with a blanket over them. If I was leaving the vehicle at her parents' house then I'd unload the guns and leave them in their hallway until I got back, then load them back up and take them home. I know, Health & Safety (and the police) would have gone mad.

But I was absolutely fascinated by the weapons and their history. At Bapty I used to get told off for getting so involved. It's just a prop, they'd say. But to me it was a piece of living history, and it was absolutely wonderful to be surrounded by the stuff all my waking hours.

To give just one example. We were preparing for the film *The Charge of the Light Brigade*, and I was cleaning up all these Enfield percussion rifles as well as some old Russian weapons. I came across a Russian Tula musket that had a little label attached to it which had clearly been written with a quill. It said: 'Russian gun, taken at Inkerman'. That was the Battle of Inkerman, during the Crimean War in 1854. And it had a sabre cut halfway down the barrel and another chunk out of the hammer spur, so you could clearly see where the soldier had lifted the gun up above his head to deflect the sabre slashes.

I sat there for hours thinking about that gun and what had happened. But for me *The Charge of the Light Brigade,* which came out in 1968, was eclipsed by another film I worked on that also came out the same year.

4

WHERE EAGLES DARE

Working as armourer alongside Richard Burton on *Where Eagles Dare* was quite a thing, but for me one of the best bits was working with Clint Eastwood. Not on the set in Austria, but back at the MGM Studios in London. Like me, he really loved motorbikes and, during the course of filming, he bought three new Norton Commandos. He got one for himself, one for Steve McQueen and one for his motorcycle mate James Garner.

Clint wanted some miles putting on the bikes to get them run in and so he asked the crew if anyone wanted to go out riding with him on a Sunday morning. Imagine the response on social media now if he asked that. But back then nobody did, nobody wanted to ride someone else's brand new bike with Clint Eastwood. Apart from me.

I had an old BSA at that point and to ride with Clint on a new Commando complete with rubber-mounted engine and, more importantly, get my fuel paid, was just fantastic. So at nine o'clock on Sunday mornings I'd be there and we'd go out and put some miles on the bikes.

I was a bit overawed to be honest, because by then he was quite iconic so I'd always let him start any conversations as I didn't really know what to talk about and didn't want to ask inane questions about *The Good, The Bad and The Ugly* or *A Fistful of Dollars* or something.

But most of the shooting time we were in Austria, in fact we were filming there for about four months and it was absolutely freezing – the snow was real. This was before materials like Goretex and I couldn't afford the really good stuff anyway so I was always cold.

And of course the guns were cold, and they don't like the cold any more than we do. They wouldn't function properly, so we'd try to keep them warm by firing off a few rounds before handing them to the actor to make sure they'd actually fire when the cameras were rolling. If it was a pistol then I'd carry it underneath my armpit to keep it warm.

Richard Burton had a bit of a problem with the pistol, a Walther PPK with a silencer. He was meant to shoot the radio operator (the late Frank Henson, known as 'Frank The Crash') in the back of the head before doing the whole 'Broadsword calling Danny Boy' scene. He had to fire a couple of shots but after the first shot the gun seemed to jam. I had a look and it seemed fine, but at the next take the same thing happened – it would fire one shot but not a second.

I took the gun and fired off several rounds and handed it back. But now I was in danger of making Richard Burton look stupid. And I realised the problem. I've found that often with a lot of actors their ability to 'emote' and do the dialogue is one thing but their physical co-ordination in tandem with the dialogue isn't very good. Richard Burton could squeeze the trigger once, but he just couldn't get the hang of releasing the trigger and squeezing it again to fire the second shot. The director, Brian Hutton, saw my look and decided we could put the second 'bang' in during post production.

Later that week, in the same corridor, there was a requirement for a big MG 42 machine gun on a tripod to be rushed in to back up the German troops, and I was 'volunteered' to be the gunner. I got kitted out, ran into the set with the gun, set it up and fired and then Clint Eastwood fired at me with the two machine pistols and I 'died'.

And they paid me more than a week's wages as an armourer for that one scene. It made me think that perhaps there was more to this 'acting/stunt' game than met the eye!

It was a magnificent, outrageous film but we overran on timings. That meant there was a scene still to be shot, where Burton and Eastwood have to rig explosive devices on a telegraph pole. It was decided to do that sequence back at MGM's studio in England. We also needed to get it done quickly because Clint Eastwood had to get back home for the birth of his child or something. Studio filming in those days wasn't quite the technological miracle it is these days.

So we had a telegraph pole set up above a high pile of 'snow', which was salt. The camera was down the bottom along with a big row of enormous lights called Brutes. These were arc lamps where two rods come together to make the light and they needed constant attention, something known as 'trimming the Brutes'. They were huge and got red hot, and needed four men just to swing them into position. A line of them meant a lot of work and heat for everyone, and everyone definitely wanted this done. We'd been working until 10pm every night to get the film finished and this was another long evening. Richard Burton had just one line to deliver, then Clint Eastwood could be gone.

But Richard Burton was pissed as a rat by that time and he was messing up the line time after time. 'Cut' they'd say wearily and try again. 'Cut.'

I was right up by the actors, looking after their guns, but even up there I sensed a change in atmosphere behind the lights. We couldn't see past the glare of the Brutes but we knew what had happened. Elizabeth Taylor had walked on set.

She was a nice lady and she'd simply come to pick up her husband. But she also had real presence and you could tell when she'd arrived simply by the change in atmosphere. Richard Burton also sensed her there and shouted out in that magnificent voice of his:

'Is that you Elizabeth?'

'Yes Richard', she answered.

'Elizabeth, I don't seem to be able to get this line right, what do you think I should do?'

There was a short pause and then Miss Taylor called out:

'Why don't you try acting you big c--t, if you know how! And then we could all get the f--k out of here.'

Everyone laughed. But since I was right up there with the actors I suppressed a giggle and stayed quiet. Burton then proceeded to deliver the line absolutely perfectly, and Eastwood could go back home.

⊙ ⊙ ⊙

There's a sad postscript to my memories of *Where Eagles Dare*. If you've seen the film then you can't forget that fantastic opening credits sequence, with the green and white camouflaged JU52 flying through the snowy mountains accompanied by the stirring Ron Goodwin soundtrack. That was actually a Swiss Air Force JU52/3m, which was later converted to civilian use after a long military career.

On 4 August 2018 the aircraft crashed during a flight in Switzerland, killing three very experienced crew and all 17 passengers.

5

SHOOTING UP WITH SIR LAURENCE

'Hello, my name is Laurence Olivier, thank you very much for coming.'
Sir Laurence on Dance of Death

There was a knock-on effect from that film. One of the stuntmen on *Where Eagles Dare* was a lovely gentle man called Max Faulkner. He was about 20 years older than me and he sort of took me under his wing. At that time it was unusual for stuntmen to treat people like armourers as anything other than a lower form of life, but he taught me about teamwork. I used to go over on my motorbike and have lunch with him and his wife and son at their house in Kensington. I worshipped Max, and he taught me a lot.

He taught me about treating people right, whatever their job. That lesson was heavily reinforced on another occasion, when I was asked to go to Twickenham Studios where I was told I'd be firing live (not blank) rounds on the set.

I stuck a selection of guns and ammo in a bag, bungeed it to the back of my motorbike and rode over to the studios, leant the bike against a wall and wandered in to see what I was meant to do, leaving the bike, guns and ammunition unattended. It was a very different world then.

They showed me into a studio where there was a framed painting of a woman on the wall of what was meant to be a 19th Century castle. They wanted to shoot holes in the painting. I was just some rocker who didn't care, so I shrugged, said it would be easy and didn't even ask about the film. Nobody nicked the guns.

I spent that morning working with a chippy making a bullet-catcher behind the painting with sleepers, sandbags and so on so that there would be no ricochets. I was happy with the results, and then lunchtime rolled around. At that point the first assistant director came down and said that we were to go upstairs to meet 'Mr Olivier' who was the star of the film, which was called *Dance of Death*.

At that point it was made abundantly clear to me that I was to address him as 'Sir Laurence', that I was to speak when spoken to and the 'couldn't care less' rocker attitude was definitely not on. By then in his career Sir Laurence Olivier was effectively God. I was ushered up to his dressing room.

Sir Laurence got up, walked over and shook my hand, saying: 'Hello, my name is Laurence Olivier, thank you very much for coming.' He went on to explain that the shot required him to go into his study, take out his revolver and, in huge frustration, shoot the painting of his wife on the wall. He explained that they'd planned to film the painting being shot as a 'cutaway' shot at the end of the day. However, Sir Laurence asked me if it might be possible to do the whole sequence in one shot and, if so, how it could be done. I was some 19-year-old shit-bubble with a leather jacket with 59 Club patches on it, and I honestly looked behind me to make sure it was me he was talking to.

I was actually confident that it could be done. Of course, now it could be done in ten minutes of post production, but even then we could have done it with explosive squibs on the painting, but they tend to spark and tear rather than make a neat hole, and he wanted it done right, and in one take.

I suggested I went up a step ladder behind the camera and to one side of Sir Laurence, with a second gun loaded with live rounds. He could then come in, and do his action which involved taking the revolver out of the desk and then turning to the painting and firing. He asked if it was safe to do this. I was perfectly confident that I could do what I'd suggested and that, as long as he wore some wax in his ears to protect them from the blast, all would be well.

I suggested that once he had his back to the camera and the revolver pointing at the painting, he could then audibly count down three, two, one, and then he'd fire the blank and I'd fire the real round over his shoulder. We ran through it with dry firing until we'd got the timing right. It seemed to work fine, so we got ready to do it for real. Health & Safety wouldn't even allow me onto the same stage with a live weapon in this day and age.

He was just a bit trepidatious, as you would be with 9mm rounds firing from behind you and 18ins from your ear, fired by a young man you don't know who's balancing up a ladder (wearing motorcycle leathers).

We did the take and it went smoothly, so he turned to the camera operator to ask if we had the shot. Back then there was no instant playback so the guy looking through the lens had to decide whether he'd got the shot or not. It was a big responsibility. But he was happy and so was Sir Laurence. He thanked me, and told me it was all my idea and all that. At which point I'm feeling ten feet tall, bulletproof and invisible, as you can imagine.

I've never forgotten that job because it was about the basis of what we do, which is teamwork. Working with him, there was no hierarchy. These days if I'm working on a film and working with an actor who I think is a bit uppity, I somehow manoeuvre that story into the mix to try to say to them they shouldn't act like an ass. Because Sir Laurence Olivier certainly didn't.

◉◉◉

My confidence in my own abilities was growing, and that's a crucial quality if you are a stuntman, which was to be the next chapter in my life. And that sense of self-belief was enhanced in a different way at about this time, while I was still working for Bapty. I was riding my motorbike past the Feltham Tyre & Rubber Company near Shepperton Studios, and I saw these big crates with Lend Lease labels on them. Being deep into all things military I wandered in and asked what was in them.

They were full of 25-pounder field gun limbers which the tyre company had bought just for the tyres. They'd taken the tyres but didn't need the rest. There were about 15 of them there and it was obvious they were now going to just sit and rot. I bought the lot. I think they were about £8 each, which meant they were a week's wages each. Which meant I didn't have the money.

But I went to Barclays Bank in the King's Road and saw the bank manager there. My mother and I had a small mortgage with them which I could wangle as collateral. I asked him to lend me £180, which at the time was a big sum of money. But he agreed, so I went back and paid for the limbers, then spent an anxious day ringing round my contacts, trying to sell them.

People realised once these were gone they were gone, and there were never going to be any more of them. One bloke bought three.

And I never actually touched any of them, as the buyers had to collect since I only had a motorbike. I can't remember how much I made but it was over 100% on the deal.

I'm not being sanctimonious but it wasn't really just about the money. There were these crates full of gun limbers complete with shell containers, spare parts wallets, everything, and I thought they're going to sit there till they fall to bits. They're historical items that should be saved – and there's a few quid to be made.

For me it was a salient lesson in opportunism. Later on when I started working for myself I used to think 'I can do that, because what you did with those field gun limbers worked out alright didn't it?'

And, let's be honest, I hate seeing things go to waste. I was brought up with rationing, and still remember standing in queues with my mother for eggs or an orange – rationing didn't end until 1954, when I was six years old. I still really hate throwing food away, even peelings. And don't get me started on 'best before' dates.

6

BROKEN BACKS AND HYPOTHERMIA

*'Right, if you just take all your clothes off
and swim out about 150 yards and lie on your face...'* Quiller *director*

You can see that in films like *The Dance of Death* and *Where Eagles Dare* I'm an armourer but I'm sort of heading towards doing a stunt.

I'd left Bapty as, like with the circus, I didn't fancy a future doing the same things for ever, even if they were fun. Then two strands came together. My mother carried on knocking me back, saying I didn't have a proper job like a solicitor or whatever she thought was a proper job, and so I thought, right, I'll show you.

And I remembered how my father had been at Arnhem as a journalist, after the battle, and he'd written articles about it and was always saying how great the Paras were. So, at 22 – much older than some recruits – I joined the Parachute Regiment. I guess I was trying to prove a point to myself, but my past as a bit of a wayward boy helped me here, as my mother had previously pushed me into an Army cadet unit, where I'd loved learning about maps, weapons, bivvies, compasses, all that stuff.

I was up against very fit 18-year-olds, but I was more experienced than them and a better shot. We had a very gruelling 16 weeks of training, and the climactic weekend of 'P' Company was the hardest thing I've ever done physically in my life. You don't know if you're going to make it but I did, and won Champion Recruit as well.

That was a real achievement for me, but I didn't really fit in. Every Friday night the boys wanted to go and get drunk and pick a fight in town and I just wasn't interested in either of those things. I got a lot of ribbing from the others but there was no way with my family background I was going to start getting drunk.

And things were so tight in the Army back then. The current kit was 1958-pattern, but we, as actual paratroopers, were only issued with the 1944-pattern kit – if you wanted the current kit you had to go and buy it yourself on the open market. And there weren't enough planes or anything else, and not much in the way of action other than Northern Ireland.

There was no way I could become an officer with my single O-level but there was an expectation with my Champion Recruit status that I'd get a stripe up fairly soon as a non-commissioned officer. But then we did a night jump over Salisbury Plain and I landed really badly and impacted vertebrae in my spine. And that was that, jump days over. They tried to get me to take a course driving trucks and stay in the army, but the CO very kindly let me be invalided out.

In 1969 there was no formal set up of stuntmen, but by 1973 when I'd been out of the Army for a year, the very first official Stunt Register was formed, and I joined it. It wasn't easy as you had to have two contracts doing stunt work to join, but I somehow pulled it all together, while driving a minicab for Greyhound Cars and doing a bit of acting as an extra – like one line on a *Doctor Who* episode – and also working as an 'ordinary' model with the aptly named Ugly Model Agency. Bills needed paying.

Once on the Register, you couldn't do any work as a film extra, you were now only allowed to do stunts, and that gave me a lean time of it for a while. But I hung in there because my life had been all over the place in the previous few years.

Together with a few others, we got a job as knockabout clowns accompanying the Evel Knievel UK tour, and we opened at Wembley Stadium with the prospect of a summer touring with the show. Evel was jumping double-decker buses, as you do. Or as he did. He was three buses short when he crashed, and that was the end of our summer 'season'.

I also began working as 'The White Knight', doing three sword fights a night at The Beefeater restaurant near The Tower of London. Coachloads of American tourists came every night to have a medieval dinner of beef and mead hosted by Henry the Eighth, with plenty of pretty serving 'wenches'. After the main meal, we would entertain sections of the punters with our sword fight. The Black Knight was Terry Richards, a 6ft 3in ex-Guardsman. He later found fame as the tall Arab swordsman who prepares to take on Indiana Jones in *Raiders of the Lost Ark,* only to be shot by an impatient Indy before the fight even began.

And then there was the Joust. Some of the more adventurous out-of-work stuntmen began jousting tournaments, which became quite popular and culminated in jousting in the moat of the Tower of London for the City of London festival. One of the groups, run by Nosher and Dinny Powell, got a contract to go over and joust in the United States and, as I could ride a horse, I was invited along. Now that was an adventure. We arrived in California at a place called Apple Valley (The Roy Rogers Museum was just down the road) where we trained the horses and took on local grooms and transport companies to shift everything up to San Francisco. That was where we opened, at a place called the 'Cow Palace', where they held indoor rodeos and Evel Knievel had just come unstuck from jumping his motorcycle (again).

It was advertised as the 'English Tourney of Knights' and we took on lots of local acts while the San Francisco Medieval Society provided pikemen and also 'wenches' to sell mead in the stands.

We were two teams, the House of York and The House of Lancaster. Our 'Queen of Light and Beauty' was Ann Sidney, who'd been Miss World in 1964. Each knight was announced and galloped into the darkened arena in the spotlight to stop before the 'queen' and announce themselves.

I was 'Sir James of Borthwick {a family name}, knight champion of Rutland'. You'd then trot off to your darkened end of the stadium where your 'groom' would hand you a lance, and you could then gently walk your horse along and choose the prettiest girl in the first four rows, and ask if you might fight for their honour and could they bestow a 'favour' for you to wear in the forthcoming joust. If they were up for it (and these were all San Francisco girls who just 'loved that British accent') they would tie their scarf or whatever (pantyhose once) to the lance and your page would then tie it to your arm. The girl would come to the stables afterwards to retrieve the item. It was a great introduction to America.

I was jousting against a guy called Jack Cooper, who was a superb rider and very competitive. We got an extra £10 for getting knocked out of the saddle so I just used to let Jack unseat me every night. With one performance every weeknight, and two on Saturdays, Sundays was a day of embrocation and feet up.

Sadly, the show went bust when the backer allegedly took the takings and buggered off to Canada, never to be seen again. I stayed on for a bit with one of the groom's family, who were very kind. It all gave me a bit of a taste for LA, so every winter after that I'd return in January or February, when the film business was quiet in England. I just rode around on Harley-Davidsons, or bought parts for my own growing collection of vintage Harleys. But I also bought the latest and best kit for stuntmen, like fire suits, pads and other equipment.

I used to stay at Phil Kaufman's place in North Hollywood. Phil was an old buddy from London days, when he had a job running the Harley-Davidson demonstration fleet He was then tour manager for various bands including the Rolling Stones and Joe Cocker. Phil was a legend in the music business as he'd been pals with Gram Parsons, who'd overdosed. They'd made a pact about funeral arrangements, so Phil borrowed a hearse and 'stole' Gram's body from the LA airport mortuary. Gram's body was being prepared to be flown back East, where, as I understand it, his hated father would have received his estate if he'd been buried there intestate.

Phil drove him out to Joshua Tree National Park and, in Phil's words, 'threw a can of five-star over him and then a match'. Someone later made a movie of it called *Grand Theft Parsons* with Johnny Knoxville playing Phil.

But behind all the fun and games my back was still unbelievably painful after the parachute accident and then the jousting. I was in the depths of depression. I just started training to keep fit and to make my spine work again. I'd go running in London with my new dog, Dodger. I suppose you could say it was quite a solitary life in the early years but I was always happy with my own company, and it teaches you to be resilient. Besides, I was always happy with Dodger. In later years he'd accompany me to every studio or stunt and sit happily by the chow wagon. When he died, 16 years after I got him, *Screen International* even printed an obituary on him.

But the odd stunt jobs started to come up and I'd grab them with both hands. I was pretty green in those days and would just go for it – these days there are all kinds of safeguards and standards to keep us safer but there weren't back then. Everyone thinks stunt work is a glamorous profession but one of my first jobs pretty much set the mark. I'm not the greatest swimmer, and I had to drown.

◉◉◉

It was for an English television spy thriller series called *Quiller*. The shot required a view as if taken from a plane of a naked dead body floating face-down in the warm waters of the Mediterranean. So they shot it off the end of Brighton Pier in February.

This was in 1974 and it was one of my first jobs, but even I wavered when they went: 'Right if you just take all your clothes off and swim out about 150 yards and lie on your face and the photographer will get the shot from the top of the pier.'

I said: 'Hang on, there's a nine-knot riptide at the end of the pier. It's February so I've got about 90 seconds before I start getting hypothermia. Where's the boat to get me there?'

And they go: 'What do you need a boat for, you're a stuntman aren't you?'

So now I'm a troublemaker. But luckily I was with another stuntman, Marc Boyle, and he sorted out a small fishing boat and we headed out to the end of the pier, him wrapped up warm and laughing happily, me all moody naked except for a dressing gown. I got the signal and went in. It was cold, properly cold, but they got the shot and I got back in the boat and back to shore, expecting some help getting my circulation going again. A girl handed me a hand towel, a tiny thing, and that's all I had. But I breathed a sigh of relief that it was done and we could get on the train back to London.

Except they went: 'Now for the second shot'. I had no idea. Although I had seen big lights further down the beach, and of course that had attracted about 150 people, mostly old ladies wrapped up warm, drawn to see what the attraction was. That was a naked me.

The bad feeling and the shivers didn't go away when I saw a fishing net, a load of very dead fish and an extra dressed up to look like a swarthy fisherman. The fish had been on the prop truck for a few days so they were falling to bits and stunk to high heaven. So now, naked, I have to wrap myself in the nylon fishing net, filled with all these dead fish and then I'm towed out into the freezing water so the fisherman can haul me in with the net.

Because I'm naked I'm getting friction burns from the nylon net as it's hauled in, and I've got bits of fish going up my nose and scales in my ears and again there's the freezing cold water. Acting dead wasn't that difficult apart from the shivering. And when I stagger out of the water the same girl hands me the same tiny towel which of course is now soaking wet from the first dunking. No hot shower or warm trailer for the stuntman!

I sat on the train to London later and finally started to warm up as I considered what kind of career this might be. Then I noticed people moving down the carriage. I was definitely warming up, and so was the smell. It must have been the whiff of glamour.

7

THE SUMMER OF '76

'And the sun never stopped shining.' Jim Dowdall

But then came the summer of 1976. Assuming you were alive, what were you doing that amazing summer? I had one of the best summers of my life, working on *The Eagle Has Landed*. The plot, if you recall, is about an elite group of German paratroopers that has a mission to come to England and kill or capture Winston Churchill. They're led by Col. Kurt Steiner, played by Michael Caine, and I was one of his small band of 'stunt' paratroopers.

We'd already filmed the 'Russian Front' stuff in Rovaniemi in Northern Finland and then been to Cornwall for a couple of weeks to do various sequences with boats and Robert Duvall (a gentleman) and some parachute stuff. Great fun with great weather. And now we're in the delightful village of Mapledurham in Oxfordshire. This is where the sequence with the mill wheel takes place, when a 'Polish' paratrooper is caught in the mill wheel and the locals see his German uniform underneath, and it all starts going wrong. The sun is shining.

I've managed to scrounge a room with a lovely couple – he's an artist – actually in the village itself, so there's no great trek to get on set, I just wander out from the walled garden and I'm there. Since moving in I've met a lovely girl who's a friend of theirs and she's moved in with me.

I have Dodger my faithful dog with me and I also own a Jeep, which is being used on the film, so I'm being paid for that as well as for my stunt work. On top of that, since things have gone well, I've bought a brand new Harley-Davidson Electra Glide and that sits gleaming in the sunshine.

And the cast is great. Michael Caine is a big star already and is so easy to work with. I really like Robert Duvall, and we sit around talking about guns and horses. Donald Sutherland, Jenny Agutter – everyone is so nice.

And then, after a day's work, there's a fantastic catering wagon which at the end of the day always has loads of salmon, steak, strawberries, whatever, left over and we can help ourselves and take it back to the walled garden for a barbecue. To avoid me getting out of shape there's also a huge gymnasium tent, but often in the evening we'll go swimming in the nearby Thames or, if the girl is there, we might go skinny dipping.

It's never got any better than those two months. And the sun never stopped shining.

⊙⊙⊙

When filming was over I regretfully planned to return to London, but instead I packed some spare underwear and a sleeping bag on the back of the Harley, left Dodger with my mother (who doted on him) and headed for Holland. As well as the other vehicles I now owned, I'd also bought a Bren Gun Carrier and that was being used on a film being made out there: *A Bridge Too Far.* I decided I needed to go and, you know, check how my vehicle was.

But the real reason was that I knew they'd have 11 Dakotas over the actual ground where the Arnhem jump happened, and they were going to recreate the drop. I just had to see that, see where my father had been. When I got there I discovered a mate of mine, Rodney Rushton, was in charge of the vehicles, and he let me crash in a spare caravan on set. Where I met a lovely Dutch girl who moved in. The sun kept shining.

Roy Button (now head of Warner Bros Europe) was second assistant director, and he knew I was ex-Bapty. He asked if I could get some of the extras knocked into shape for the big scene of the crossing of the Waal River by teaching them just some of the basics of weapon handling. This was a boat crossing under fire, known as Cook's Crossing. Robert Redford was flying in for just ten days filming, playing the part of Major Cook. But this was the Seventies and he refused to get his hair cut. If you look closely you can see his hair is tucked up underneath his helmet. He had to have a light wooden rifle too as he felt he didn't look athletic enough carrying a real, heavy one.

The Waal is a major waterway but the Dutch authorities had agreed to shut it between 8am and 9am on a Sunday morning. We had one hour. We'd been up and ready since 2am as there was so much to organise. There were so many people that catering just wasn't going happen so we were hungry and a bit weary before it even started. And Robert Redford was late.

Eventually we got going. We were all in the boats, and we knew that on the opposite bank there was a great big 1000mm camera lens. I was in one of the lead boats, in uniform, firing away, and beside me was one of the special effects guys. He had explosive charges which he was letting out on a rope into the water. When they were reasonably near 'Major Cook' he would set them off, to look like incoming mortar and artillery fire. Except we were a bit fed up, and encouraged him to let the charges out a bit more, a bit closer to Robert Redford's boat.

When they went up it was like a bath was dumped on him, but he knew he had this big lens on him and he had to keep going. We were all sitting ahead of him, firing away and laughing our bollocks off.

⊙⊙⊙

That was fun, but it wasn't what I was there for. And I did see the drop. I was down on the ground and they were landing all around me and it was absolutely fantastic. I was wearing a German uniform and firing up at the British Paras and the extras around me were doing the same. Because I'd taught them how to do it.

I'd seen the German extras earlier and they'd been practising firing blanks up at the paratroopers, but they'd been messing around, trying to balance stones on the end of the barrels and then firing them, thinking it was funny. Years later that experience stood me in good stead when the Russian extras I had to train on *Enemy at the Gate* showed a similar propensity for messing around, although they had the added handicap of very often suffering massive hangovers from their vodka consumption the previous evening (see Chapter 14). I showed the Dutch 'Germans' what I'd later show the Russians.

I got a melon and put the rifle muzzle up against it and pulled the trigger. This was just with blanks, but you don't get a melon with a hole in it, you get a vapourised melon. I pointed out that a blank round can blow a hole in your foot or hand if you don't treat the weapon with respect. The Dutch 'German' extras stopped messing about in Holland and the Russian 'Russian' extras in Germany did the same although I did have to send a couple of really drunk guys home again before we started.

After a couple of weeks in Holland, I loaded up the Harley and rode home a very happy man. Because I'd been working with extras and stunt guys, they'd had to pay me as a stuntman, so I was probably the highest paid extra on that film. And the Bren Gun Carrier was fine. And the sun kept shining.

8

A SHORT LIST OF INJURIES – THERE ARE OTHERS

'Stupid boy' Captain Mainwaring, Dad's Army

That all sounds like the most wonderful Boy's Own stuff, and quite often it was. And sometimes it wasn't. Being a stuntman is all about reducing risk, but you're still taking a risk, even if you figure the percentage is acceptably low. And sometimes it goes wrong, no matter how much you've rehearsed it, how often you've run over what could go wrong and worked to eliminate the errors.

Being set on fire; falling out of buildings; being in car crashes; falling off motorbikes – all the things a sensible person might have nightmares about, I've done.

I've had some burns from the fire jobs, I've got damaged vertebrae at the base of my spine from my parachuting accident plus three more in my neck from *Superman 2.* In that film, apart from being injured in the White House corridor sequence, I also played the part of a Russian astronaut on the surface of the Moon who is picked up by Terence Stamp and hurled off into space. The visor of my helmet kept popping open as I went upside down so they taped it shut just before the take. This gave me about two minutes of breath but a couple of times I was 'out' when they brought me down! I've broken my nose three times and fractured my skull twice. On one occasion, filming in Denmark, the stunt went wrong and I got an arrow right through my leg. The local hospital remarked they hadn't seen an injury like it for about 400 years.

Earlier in my stunt career I agreed to jump out of a second-floor window. That's no big deal but, with another stuntman (Marc Boyle again), I had to jump, land on concrete and then run away since we were burglars escaping the police. It was about a 12ft drop and we did it fine but afterwards the continuity girl came up and told us they'd felt the impact through the concrete even where they'd been standing.

She reckoned we'd know about it once we were old, but when you're that age you just don't think about it. I do now. Knees are buggered.

Often it's not the big dramatic scenes where you get hurt. In one I was doubling for Private Pike in *Dad's Army*. The Home Guard has found a butterfly bomb up a telegraph pole and Pike has to get it down. They commandeer a passing lorry full of second-hand furniture and they build up the furniture on top of the lorry so Pike can clamber up and reach the bomb. The idea is that as he nears the top the whole tottering pile falls over and Pike lands amusingly in a nearby midden. Ho ho and home for tea.

The pile of furniture was about 12ft on the flatbed of the lorry so it was quite high. It was rigged so in theory it would topple to one side, and that was where I'd built the 'midden', a bed of cardboard boxes with straw and stuff over the top. I wasn't convinced the furniture would collapse properly but the special effects guy seemed convinced and I was relatively new to the game so I went for it.

In the event the tower of furniture just whiplashed so, instead of falling sideways into the midden, I dropped straight down. I just missed the side of the truck, which would have really bust me up, and crashed down beside it. Then a wardrobe, an actual wardrobe from the pile, landed on my head. I was completely unconscious for a minute or two. I went to the hospital and they found a hairline fracture in my skull but there wasn't much they could do about it. I still get repeat fees when they show that episode on television but I had dizzy spells and a sore neck for days.

And then on *Superman 2* in 1980 I had a second really bad fall. I was one of the White House staff when the villains burst through the skylight and there's a very one-sided fight. I got thrown over one of their heads by Sarah Douglas and then I flew through the air upside-down before colliding with stuntman Bill Weston. That was the plan – it takes just a few seconds in the film.

It's two shots. First, me flying up and overhead, which is done by a teeter board, where two blokes jump on one end of a see-saw and I then fly off the other. That went fine but the second shot is me flying through the air upside down before colliding with Bill Weston. For that I had to jump onto a mini trampoline and get enough momentum that I went forward hard as well as up. We rehearsed it a lot.

The trampoline shifted slightly as I hit it.

I didn't realise. I flew through the air upside down and got the height but I didn't get the distance I needed. Unfortunately the stuntman was braced for my impact and didn't see I was falling short. I landed on the back of my head. I hit that studio floor so hard. I've got three damaged vertebrae at the top of my neck as a result and really that's given me trouble all my life since, with headaches and pains in my shoulders and neck.

So you do everything to avoid things going wrong. You prepare, rehearse, check, double-check and treble-check. As I'm fond of repeating: 'Assumption is the mother of all foul-ups'. Or words to that effect.

Some of that is just practical preparation, but am I superstitious? Yes I am. I always put my left boot on first, all that stuff with magpies and ladders! Let's just say that I'm conscious of certain paraphernalia that I like to have with me, and conscious of not doing little things that could be interpreted as something that could bring bad luck later on.

Before a big job like a full burn or a car turn-over I never want to hear someone wishing me good luck. Because a couple of times people have said that and it's all gone slightly wrong. In the minutes before a big job you need to just go inside yourself and run through every single detail again and again. It's a sort of Zen moment where you need to concentrate on what you are about to do, and ask yourself if you feel lucky and if you feel confident you can do this.

And you're always aware there's a lot of pressure for you to just get on with it and do the stunt. A lot of people, money and everything else are waiting just for you. At that point you have to really believe in your own capabilities and your own judgement. Occasionally that means not going ahead, having another look, a think about another way to do things. Like on *Hanover Street*.

In this wartime romance there's a wire-and-batten bridge that goes across a huge chalk quarry about 90ft up in the air. Christopher Plummer and Harrison Ford are running across it when a tank fires a shell that blows the bridge in two. Christopher Plummer is near where it breaks and clings on as part of the bridge falls away. That was the plan, and I was doubling for Christopher Plummer.

The bridge was going to break when they fired explosive bolts either side of the wire-and-batten structure. These were just industrial exploding bolts, bought off the shelf. I was reassured it would all be fine and could we get on with it, but since I was going to be about five feet from where they exploded I insisted on a dry run as it was my arse that was going to be so close to the bang. To much tutting and sighing from Sfx, I asked for steel caps to be put over the bolts so they'd be contained. Special Effects declined.

The bridge duly blew and the two halves dropped away, anchored at the ends. Everyone went off for lunch. Except me. I walked in circles down in the quarry, searching the ground. Eventually I found what I was looking for and went and dragged the special effects guy away from his lunch. I showed him. I'd found one of the boltheads about 140 yards away. Granted it had fallen from a height, but it had still been fired with considerable force a considerable distance.

We decided on the spot that they'd weld some covers over the exploding boltheads. I've still got that bolthead somewhere in my 'Black Museum'. It's about trusting your own instincts when you're not happy with something even though there's huge pressure not to make a fuss and just get on with it. I'm sure many people can relate to that in normal life. (Interestingly, it was the same special effects guy who was responsible for my coming unstuck on the *Dad's Army* gag.)

You have to listen to your own experience because there's no replacement for experience in our business – or any business – so you need to listen to what the old ones tell you, particularly the ones who have been hurt.

Oh, that's me then.

9

STAR WARS

You have to remember that in 1977 there was no mystique around *Star Wars,* at least when it was being made. For me it was just a job with a lot of running around in uncomfortable outfits. It was like another episode of *Doctor Who* or *Blake's* 7, with floppy sets and bits of plastic costume that dug into you if you tried to sit down. Or so we thought.

I was a stunt stormtrooper on the original film, so if someone was going to get shot, hit or blown up, it was one of a small cadre of stuntmen, of which I was one. There were plenty of others running around in the white armoured suits, but they didn't have to hurt themselves. Lucky them.

The outfits looked great, but they were made of plastic and it was incredibly hot inside, even before you started running about the place. There were sharp bits everywhere, so when you had to fall over it really hurt. And the helmet would move on your head. You'd find yourself only able to see the roof or the floor, so we had to pack the helmets out with foam rubber to keep them in place – and that of course made them hotter than ever.

The worst bit was hanging around between takes. They'd tell us to just go and stand over there, it'll only be for a couple of minutes. It was actually half an hour, but they didn't want us taking the helmets off as it was such a palaver to get them back on again. We poured buckets of sweat out of those outfits.

And it all seemed so daft to us. We just didn't get it. We had to run around with Sterling sub-machine guns which had been converted to have only short five-round magazines. Which meant we were endlessly having to reload to fire the blanks. We couldn't see the point of that at all.

You may have gathered that the stunt crew weren't exactly enamoured of the film. But at least Harrison Ford, who was running around being all butch all over the place, was okay to work with and Carrie Fisher was very polite, very nice to everyone. And the late Peter Mayhew, the Yorkshireman who played Chewbacca, was a really lovely, gentle man.

At that time Harrison Ford was starting to become a really big deal as an actor, and it was interesting to watch. Once they become recognised in the street, actors tend to go one of two ways. They can become very welcoming, saying hello to everyone, signing all the autographs and so on, but that becomes immensely time-consuming.

Or they withdraw, and that can come over – fairly or unfairly – as if they've put themselves on a slightly higher plane than everyone else. That's hard to deal with when you're interacting with them, which is why for most of my career I've steered clear of trying to chat and socialise with the big stars. But the stars on *Star Wars* were all just fine.

The film got made and I moved on to other things and pretty much forgot about it until I got a ticket for the crew showing. It was on at the Odeon in Tottenham Court Road in London on a Saturday morning so I hopped on my motorbike and headed down there. But then it started to rain, really pour and I thought about turning round and going home – I didn't really care about seeing the film. But I figured I wasn't going to get any drier if I turned round, so I carried on.

There were some bored crew and stuntmen there and we settled in, more interested in the Dolby Sound which the cinema had installed as we'd never experienced it before. Then we saw that opening sequence with the ship coming over from the top of the screen, with that Dolby sound. Wow. At the end of that sequence we all stood up and applauded and told each other it couldn't get any better than that.

Then we saw the stormtroopers and we wondered how the hell they'd done those laser blasts and strikes. Remember this was in the 1970s and we'd been running about in front of a blue screen, which didn't tell us anything. We had no idea. Then it started to make sense that they'd been so insistent exactly when and in what direction we fired the blanks from those Sterlings.

What they'd been doing was simply looking for the muzzle flash. Then, with the sort of technology that was completely new to us at that time, they'd replaced that flash in post production with the laser blast. It must have taken forever to do with some of those battles, but the effect was like nothing we'd ever seen before.

Then there's the scene where Princess Leia is a hologram – and we'd never seen one of those before either. At the end we all stood up and applauded all over again – and that doesn't happen often. I rode back home and spent the rest of the day ringing everyone and telling them they had to go and see this fantastic new film called *Star Wars*.

That was in 1977, with the film that came to be called *A New Hope*. The follow-up, *The Empire Strikes Back*, came out three years later, and once again I was running around in uncomfortable outfits. I wasn't complaining this time.

I also had a little cameo role as a Bespin Guard. I'm guarding Harrison and Carrie but they break out and smack me round the head with my own pistol. I fall down, haha etc and home for tea. I didn't think anything of it, but that small stunt has led to people writing to me from all over the world.

After more than 40 years, *Star Wars* is making more money than ever, it's such a fabulous franchise. And one aspect is that the fans pay attention to every single character, no matter how large or small. Somewhere I've got a plastic figure in a box who's based on my Bespin Guard. People have come up with a whole back story for the guy, complete with what planet he came from, what his name was – Jared I think - and loads of other stuff.

About seven years ago I got a phone call out of the blue asking if I'd like to come and sign autographs at a *Star Wars* convention at Olympia in London. I genuinely thought they'd got the wrong guy, and I wasn't really interested, but they offered me a good day rate and I wasn't doing anything else so I went along.

I bumped into a few old mates including the mother and daughter stunt pair of Sadie and Tracey Eden and some others, and thought it might be a fun day after all, even though I didn't think anyone would want a lowly autograph like mine. The event opened at 10am and they opened the doors.

We were sitting at tables and I was feeling a bit foolish, so I wasn't ready for the absolute cascade of people pouring through the doors. Honestly it was like this fast-moving tidal wave charging towards us. They were lined up six deep in front of the tables in no time.

The very first bloke unrolls this official poster with lots of signatures on. He knew he didn't have mine. I noticed his accent so asked him where he was from. He was from Sydney he said, and I said, 'What, Australia?' He nodded. He was there for one day but he simply had to get the autographs that he was missing.

The second bloke also had an accent and it turns out he was from Austin, Texas, and he'd come to England just to attend this convention. I was absolutely amazed. I signed over 100 autographs that day. And saw people paying for it. So now I have my own photographs, some coloured Sharpies because some people are quite specific about particular ink colours for the signature, and I do selfies with people and all sorts.

It's just a massive, massive thing and I'd had no idea. I went to one such event in Japan about ten years ago and every single person was in some sort of *Star Wars* costume. Apart from me.

1   *Doubling for Roger Moore, on Octopussy,
under the Nene Valley steam train.*

2   *On Octopussy. The train's at
45mph and the bridge is solid.*

3   *A moody young man, in the early years of stunt work*

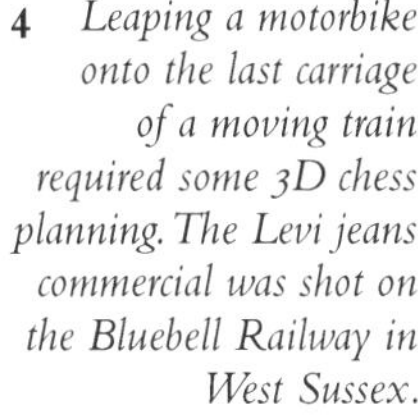

4   *Leaping a motorbike
onto the last carriage
of a moving train
required some 3D chess
planning. The Levi jeans
commercial was shot on
the Bluebell Railway in
West Sussex.*

5   *Sean Connery and Catherine Zeta-Jones – I had to keep them safe filming on* Entrapment. Photo credit: David Appleby/Universal Pictures.

6   *Training Catherine Zeta-Jones to do a wire-assisted walk over a12ft high beam on* Entrapment, *which took a bit of rehearsing.* Photo credit: David Appleby/Universal Pictures.

7 *Risk can equal reward. Some of my toys and my Harris hawk 'Smartie' in the early 1990s.*

8 *A TV commercial shot in Zambia for a Panasonic video camera meant I had to get very close to a rhino that wasn't quite ready for its close-up.*

9   Octopussy. *All I had to do was jump from the speeding car to the train.* Photo credit: Danjaq SA.

10   *Reversing the Jeep as a landing pad for Steve Griffin's car flip on* GoldenEye.

11   *The first time I met my then picture prop BMW R75 on the set of* The Dirty Dozen. *I managed to buy it after* A Bridge Too Far. *One of my favourite bikes and desired by, but not sold to, Brad Pitt many years later on* Fury.

12   *The BMW once it was safely in my possession got a smart new paint job.*

13 On Octopussy. *With stuntman Martin Grace badly injured, I've just put on Roger Moore's outfit and am preparing to clamber around the train. A pensive moment.*

Photo credit: Marc Hernandez.

14 *With stuntman Julian Spencer and 'the kids' on* The Borrowers. *I had the airbag specially constructed with a very soft top to make the landing as gentle as possible for the kids.*

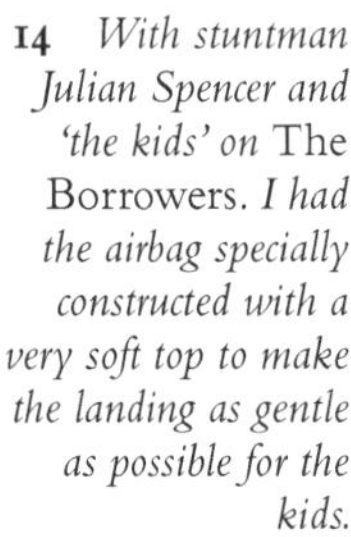

15 Doubling Christopher Plummer on 'Hanover Street' with a really bad wig, along with stuntman Del Baker.

16 On The Eagle Has Landed, *in Finland. I'm freezing second-left. Stuntman Del Baker once again to my right.*

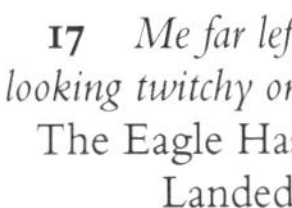

17 Me far left looking twitchy on The Eagle Has Landed.

18 *On Hanover Street I was doubling for Christopher Plummer, chasing Harrison Ford across a bridge. A tank shell blows it in half and I was left hanging on to the broken bridge. It was about 90ft in the air.*

19 *The initial bang involving the exploding bolt!*

20 *Just before dropping to the last rung.*

21 *Hanging in there.*

10

FLASH GORDON

'What do you mean, "Flash Gordon approaching"?' Kala

About the same time we were shooting *The Empire Strikes Back* I was heavily involved in another space opera. *Flash Gordon* came out in 1980, and it's fair to say it didn't get off to an auspicious start for me.

I was on board for doing some of the stunts but, while that was going on, I also went to audition for a part in the film. The problems started the evening before the audition. I was at a dinner party with about eight or nine of us, including the father of the hostess. The meal, like the 1970s, was coming to an end when the hostess brought out a plate of chocolate brownies. I ate three. So did the old father.

Yup, they were those sort of chocolate brownies. About an hour and a half later I was completely off my head. Actually I don't understand why people want to do drugs or drink, the loss of control felt frightening to me. I just wanted it to stop, but it didn't. I have no idea how the father of the hostess got on, but by the next morning I was a wreck and had to call a mate to drive me to the casting.

The casting lady was a bit of a legend called Mary Selway, something of a toughie at the best of times. And, somehow, these weren't the best of times. The day before I'd rung and spoken to her assistant to make my mark and we'd got on great, so I was hoping she would be behind the desk.

I got up to the first floor, and there was the casting office at the end of a long corridor. There were lots of doors either side and they all had names on and the film logo. And I stopped at every single door and marvelled loudly at how wonderful the logos were and how clever it all was. All the colours and patterns looked so beautiful. People were sticking their heads out in the corridor, wondering what all the kerfuffle was about.

Eventually I got to the end door, knocked on it and breezed in. There was someone behind the desk and I launched into some spiel, the full 'hello darling' nonsense. I told her I was there to see Mary Selway and got an icy reply that she *was* Mary Selway.

The only good news was that I was auditioning to be one of the Hawkmen, who were dressed in a pair of tiny shorts and some moody feathers and wings and not much more. She asked me to take my shirt off and I went 'Oooh, you are saucy' (as per Benny Hill). It really wasn't going well.

But I was training and doing weights and really built in those days, so that bit went okay, and then, since the part needed me to fly on wires, she asked if I'd ever flown before. And I said: 'You should try to be where I am right now.'

I didn't get the part…

But actually one of the Hawkmen got injured later so I did get to fly, only this time with a clear head. We had to fly around this huge cold aircraft hanger in Weybridge suspended by two single-strand piano wires so the wire wouldn't show up to the cameras. If one of the wires broke, as they sometimes did, then it was only a matter of time before the other one snapped too. They made a horrid noise.

Which was fairly rough, as we were suspended up to 30ft above the floor. We had a huge bed of cardboard boxes underneath us but it was still a big fall. The real issue was that we weren't wearing very much, it was freezing cold and after about ten minutes hanging up there you'd start to get 'harness trauma' which was about as much fun as it sounds. Your legs would go to sleep, and there were various other unpleasantnesses to be endured.

One big hold-up was caused by a stunt man, who had to be shot as he appeared on a balcony below us. He had to press a button to set off the explosive hit on his body and then fall over the balcony onto the box bed below. The problem was his co-ordination, or lack of it.

The three elements of setting off the hit, staggering from the wound and then falling off the balcony were just beyond him. We hung up there for ages while he'd remember one or two steps of the sequence but not all three, or not in the right sequence. Eventually he appeared at the balcony, staggered as if hit and went over the balcony and fell into the bed of boxes.

Then he remembered he hadn't pressed the button for the hit and did so as he lay there. The resulting small explosion set all the boxes on fire. So then everyone had to wade in there and drag him out through all these burning cardboard boxes. We agreed to cut that scene in the end.

But that still left a really big fight scene between Prince Barin and Flash Gordon. The two are locked in combat while balancing on this disc-shaped platform. That in turn revolves and moves around, while knives pop up and down from its surface. In the film all this is controlled by a roaring Brian Blessed. I was doubling for Timothy Dalton who played Barin, while my mate Rocky Taylor was doubling for Sam Jones, who played Flash Gordon.

That one fight was so complicated we rehearsed it for two weeks. We also had to fight with bullwhips so we had to get an expert in to teach us. Reg Harding was an ex-rodeo cowboy and he taught us what is a real art. He was there training us up for a whole week, but we got it eventually. It's definitely not as easy as it looks!

Every day we were rehearsing the moves because we wanted to get it done in one big master shot. Some of it was simply being thrown onto the floor. The idea was that the knives would draw back into the floor just as we were landing, so timing was really important. The knives were made of rubber but, to stop them flopping about, they had a steel core, so you really didn't want to land on one.

The disc used for the shoot was this really exotic thing which moved and tipped as if floating in space, but we rehearsed with a simple disc on the ground so we could get each move perfect. I'd been working hard and managed to put my embarrassing incident with Mary Selway out of my mind, but somehow I almost managed to put my foot in it again.

There were the two of us stuntmen and the fight co-ordinator Bill Hobbs, and that was meant to be it, otherwise an empty stage so we could focus. But this little guy kept turning up. He didn't say anything but he'd just watch us. He always wore this slightly down-at-heel suit and he started to get on my nerves, so I complained to Bill about him hanging around like a bad smell.

Then they told me that was Dino de Laurentiis, the producer of *Flash Gordon* and one of the most famous film producers ever. I began to wonder if I'd get the stunt done before they threw me and my mouth off the film.

However, when it came time to do the fight for real it went really well and all that hard work paid off. But in the last bit of the fight I got kicked over the edge of the disc and had to hang on the lip. Unfortunately as I went over the edge and down I smashed into a big heavy lamp with my back. I let go and fell into the rig but I took some of the lamp with me, which then landed on me. I was hurting pretty badly but I knew we'd at least got the sequence.

I think that was also the last time I ate a chocolate brownie.

11

FROM THUNDERBALL TO OCTOPUSSY

'And All Because The Lady Loves …'
Milk Tray Chocolate ad, 1980s

James Bond and I go back, way back to 1965 and *Thunderball*. I've been working on Bond films for the better part of 40 years and I can get all professional and technical about them but really most of them were the most amazing fun. They had the biggest budgets, the biggest villains, the biggest explosions – they were just the biggest and best.

It was almost like a big family gathering. Every 18 months or so we'd all get together somewhere exotic – and then blow it up. I think I've done about eight or nine Bond films, starting with *Thunderball* and then the first *Casino Royale* a couple of years later, which was a bit of a send-up with Peter Sellers.

But it was *The Spy Who Loved Me* in 1977 when it all went really huge. This was the film where a supertanker swallows a submarine, and the organisers soon realised there wasn't a film set in the entire world that would be large enough. But producer Cubby Broccoli didn't shrink his ideas, instead he said we'll build the set ourselves.

The set designer was Sir Ken Adam, a lovely man who'd been born in Germany in the 1920s but, as a Jew, he'd escaped to England where he became a fighter pilot flying Typhoons. Anyway, he built this incredible set which, at the time, was the largest sound set in the world. Stanley Kubrick did the lighting. That was how big Bond was becoming.

But the reality was the film needed a lot of stuntmen and, at that time, the Stunt Register was only a few years old, and quite a lot of the people on it were WWII veterans. There was a requirement for a cadre of younger guys, which included me.

It sound so glamorous, but as ever the film was shot in January and February and it was freezing. It really was bitter cold and we had to fall into the water, roll around on the concrete and generally get beaten up. The film used just about every stuntman on the Register, and actually we had a ball.

It was similar on *For Your Eyes Only* (1981), when they took about 30 stunt guys out to Greece to have an absolutely massive punch-up on a boat. Then we stayed on for a few days and some of us got bit parts – I ended up being a guard up at the monastery. That was a mighty fine way to earn good money, but what really sticks in my mind is the stunt performed by Rick Sylvester.

This American stuntman was doubling for Roger Moore, and he had to climb up this cliff, which was shot at one of the Meteora monasteries. It was a huge and steep climb, then, when he got near the top, a baddy kicked him off and he fell about 30ft until the rope he was wearing pulled him to a stop.

Naturally, that rope couldn't just jerk tight after a fall of that height or it would have severely damaged him. Back then there weren't all the trick kinds of kit we have now to decelerate so Rick had to work out a system for himself. It was very clever and involved a series of sandbags in a trough spaced about six inches apart. A rope was fed through each one and then knotted on the other side of a large washer on the last sandbag. When the rope tightened as he fell, the sandbags slammed into each other successively from the top and, as the whole pull became heavier and heavier, the rope came to a final decelerating stop. Simple but effective. It worked but I remember watching it and thinking 'rather you than me mate'.

I well remember thinking at the time that the kind of 'fan descender' that had been used in the Army for parachute training would have been a better way of doing it. Not so many years later that idea was put into practice, and has become a standard safety rig for some high falls.

By the time of *Octopussy* a couple of years later, Roger Moore was still going strong and the lovely Irishman Martin Grace was doubling for him during a hair-raising fight on top of a train. I was doubling the baddy, Gobinda, which meant I had to be blacked up with a beard and turban every day – that's just not something that would happen in today's PC environment.

It was meant to be shot on top of a steam train in India, but actually we used the 19th Century Nene Valley Railway in Cambridgeshire.

(It got used again in *GoldenEye*.) There was nothing clever about the scene, we were up there at about 45mph having a real fight which was being filmed from a helicopter.

The tricky bit was that there was a brick bridge along the route that was only about 18 inches higher than the roof of the train, so one of us had to be always facing the direction of travel. As we thundered towards the bridge the one facing it had to keep fighting but call out a countdown from three. At 'one' we'd both fall flat as the bridge whooshed over us. Then we'd stand up and continue. That was all for real.

If we'd got that wrong it would have been game, set and match. It was hairy but it went well. Then Martin as Bond had to do some filming clambering about down the side of the train. Which is where it all went very wrong.

We were going up and down a particular section of track as we needed to avoid bridges and other obstacles that came very close to the side of the train further down the line. There was an agreed stopping point, because obviously it was too dangerous to go further with Martin hanging on the side of the train. Somehow there was a misunderstanding between the crews on the train and the helicopter, and the train kept going past the agreed stop point.

Martin was busy acting on the side of the train when he hit a concrete wall at about waist height. Somehow he managed to hang on – if he'd let go he'd probably have gone under the wheels. But he hung on until the train stopped, and then he fell.

He'd broken his pelvis in several places and he could see his thigh bone through the great gash in his leg. Martin was on the stretcher in absolute agony with me walking alongside him – starting to take off the 'Bond' wig.

He understood what I was doing and told me to take it. With him out, I was going to have to finish the sequence and we only had one Bond wig. From then on it was me down the side of the train and then underneath it, my face about six inches off the rails. Martin was in hospital for months but we got the filming done.

Martin Grace was the original 'man in black' in those old Cadbury's Milk Tray ads of the 1980s. While he was in hospital a lot of people brought him chocolates.

12

BROSNAN AS BOND

'Be good to people, be kind to people, show up,
read the lines, hit the mark, and go home.' Pierce Brosnan

Back in the 1970s I'd been feeding a future Bond. Pierce Brosnan was at the Camden Drama Centre, where I used to go and teach a bit of unarmed combat with a mate of mine. Afterwards we'd take the young Brosnan out for beans on toast because he didn't have any money in those days.

I didn't see him for about ten years, then went to see him on the set of *Remington Steele* in the US. I was out buying bits for my Harley-Davidson, buying new stunt kit as they had the best stuff, and generally avoiding an English winter with little work. The last time I'd seen him he'd been a penniless actor in London and there I was gawping at this absolutely enormous trailer. And he grins and goes 'Yeah, good isn't it?'.

Roll forward to 1995 and we're reunited again on the set of *GoldenEye*, the first of the four Bond films he starred in. Continuing the theme of my glamorous life, I had an acting part in the film. I was a Russian soldier sitting on the toilet, reading the paper, then I get knocked out – 'Beg your pardon, forgot to knock'.

I have to say, one of the greatest stunts – or 'gags' as we call them – was done by Wayne Michaels. You'll probably remember the opening sequence where, as Bond, he dives off a dam. It was the longest bungee jump from a solid structure ever attempted in a film. He fell over 700ft, straight down, reaching more than 100mph. Not only that, but as he slowed, he had to draw a gun, which threw him off trajectory.

He did it perfectly, and that let Bond into the Russian building complex, which let him then take out me and some other Russian soldiers. But actually I did have a bit more to do with the film than sit around with my trousers down getting punched in the face. They'd brought me in because of my knowledge of military vehicles. There was the tank sequence.

GoldenEye was the first film shot at the new Leavesden Studios in Hertfordshire, which aren't far from the Elstree Studios. It had been an aerodrome and had made Handley Page Halifax heavy bombers and De Havilland Mosquitos during WWII, but had been abandoned after Rolls-Royce stopped producing helicopters there in the early 1990s. The huge hangars made the perfect location for a Bond film studio.

Barbara Broccoli, daughter of Cubby, was the producer and she wanted to shoot much of the film in St Petersburg in Russia. But they couldn't agree to all the fees, so she had St Petersburg built in Hertfordshire so we could shoot in both locations. Which meant the tank sequences were going to be shot in both Russia and England.

Rule Number One: Make Yourself Invaluable.

Before filming started I'd put myself through a tank driving course in England, so that I knew all there was to know about driving and looking after the T-55. Certainly before any filming took place in St Petersburg we had to get the tank sorted. Or tanks, should I say.

We had three. One was brand new, complete with manuals, snorkel kit, the works. The second was a bit knackered but okay, and the third had come from the Israeli Defence Forces. It had clearly seen action – I found live 7.62 rounds amid the sand in the bottom of it.

The issue was that we had to make the tank look like a T-72. On top of that, the Russian authorities had made it plain that if we were going to drive a tank down their streets it had to have rubber treads on the tracks, so as not to cause too much damage. That was a problem right there since the T 55 doesn't come with rubber treads.

However, getting together with the special effects guys, we worked out that Chieftain tracks, which have rubber blocks, would just about fit. I bought tons of Chieftain track and then spent days with a gas axe cutting off the horns so it would just fit. We also needed new cast drive sprockets at the back.

We now had a tank that could roll on rubber. Gary Powell was the principal tank driver, so I taught him how to drive the thing. He was absolute mustard at the controls. It could turn quite sharply as it had a two-speed axle, and that was good as we wanted the tank to slide around. But with the grippy rubber pads it simply wouldn't.

So I spent days driving the tanks around, wearing down the rubber pads. Then we experimented with buckets of water and diesel on the road surface, then water and washing-up liquid – anything that would help the tank break traction. Eventually we found a formula that worked. Now for one of the big scenes.

This was where a car comes sliding sideways into view just as the wall behind it explodes and the tank comes flying through. This was not CGI, this was real. We worked out that the tank would need to be at full speed, about 35mph, which meant we needed a run-up distance of about three quarters of a mile. At that point the tank's flat out, going up a ramp of sleepers towards a solid wall of breeze blocks, and bursts through just as the villain's car slides around the corner and the tank begins the pursuit.

That took some bottle as obviously tank driver Gary Powell was just looking at a wall getting rapidly closer, and couldn't see a thing the other side. That was my job. I was running the floor which meant co-ordinating the timings, so I had to count the car in, giving it time to four-wheel drift sideways into the shot, while this huge tank was thundering up the ramp unseen behind it. That also took some bottle on the part of Steve Street, the driver of the car. He didn't want the car to hesitate or cut out at that point.

We'd rehearsed and rehearsed, and on the day everyone was fantastic and it worked perfectly. That was a big stunt and I sighed with relief when it was done. But not all the stunts went that smoothly.

In another one the tank crashes into a Perrier lorry, and we decided we needed a car to come across between the two, just to add a bit of extra movement and tension. The driver of the car was hidden down a sidestreet, so he couldn't see the tank barrelling along at 30mph. He was entirely dependent on my signal to go from standstill to as fast as he could, to zip out of that sidestreet and get across before the tank got there, on its way to hit the Perrier lorry.

The car driver was Eddie Kidd. He'd done some of the most amazing motorcycle jumps and stunts and held a lot of world records. He's a really lovely, nice man with balls of steel, but he had a bit of an issue with concentration. I thought I'd finally got him to focus. I was standing there, watching the tank coming down the road fast, watching the lorry, and then I gave Eddie the countdown from three to go. I was quite tense. But then I gave him the signal to go and realised he wasn't even looking at me, he was chatting to someone else!

Then he noticed and launched the car. I was waving my arms and shouting into the radio to abort but he was going now. He came out of that sidestreet right in front of 48 tons of steel moving at 30mph. He made it, just. He just laughed afterwards when I pointed out he was seconds away from being killed.

(Sadly Eddie had a life-changing accident some years later, but he hasn't let it stop him – he's completed a London Marathon which he had to start and finish in a wheelchair.)

Anyway, that whole stunt really aged me. It's no wonder I have so many grey hairs. But first, we went to St Petersburg.

That didn't get any simpler when it turned out that one of the streets we wanted to use was simply out of bounds for a full battle tank as it was too heavy. So we got together with the special effects guys. We took a British Saladin armoured car and they built a totally convincing dummy T-72 body over it, complete with tracks that actually went round. I drove that in the places a real tank wasn't allowed - but the real tanks were still causing problems.

The issue was that we'd rigged up a small camera under the gun barrel and another pair either side so the driver was looking at three tiny screens. But that's so two-dimensional that I for one found it really difficult to place the tank with any accuracy. That's not what you need when you're in a street with people, where someone 10 feet away looks about 40 feet away. I decided we had to cut out a bit of the glacis plate on the front and fit some Perspex and then camouflage it. Simple idea.

Except of course this is really thick steel designed to stop a tank shell. I spent a whole day and about five bottles of gas cutting out a small square, which was immensely thick and heavy – I still use it as a doorstop at home. But at least now we could drive the tank with some confidence that we weren't going to kill people.

Just one of those little strange quirks of filming: There's a scene where the tank runs over a police car, with two policemen in it. We were towing the car, which had dummies inside, and the tank loomed up behind and duly ran right over it, crushing it to pulp. But if you want a lower-age certificate for the whole film, you must show that the occupants weren't killed, so we had to include a scene of the two men crawling from the wreckage.

We were firing cars into the canal with our stunt guys in them, and there were small icebergs in that canal. Some of the Russian stunt guys had to get hit by cars and be thrown into the water. I was talking to them and realised they didn't have any of the kit we used, like special pads on knees and elbows and so on. They just had bits of carpet underfelt taped to their arms.

I worked with some of them years later on *The Bourne Supremacy* in Moscow and by then they were happy to show me they'd got some decent kit, including pads.

The big statement vehicle in the next franchise, *Tomorrow Never Dies*, wasn't a tank, but the latest BMW saloon. The trick was that the BMW 750i could be remotely controlled by a mobile phone, which in 1997 was a really exciting thought. I believe Ericsson sold a ton of the JB988 phones once the film came out – although you had to supply your own BMW.

But it also meant that the car had to be driven about with nobody visible at the wheel. Which meant that the main driver, Steve Street (who'd been driving the villains' car in *GoldenEye*), was squatting down behind the driver's seat with a black drape over him. Once again, he was looking through a small screen, with the controls extended under the driver's seat. He did an outstanding job as he sat there staring at a tiny 2D screen, power sliding the BMW round this underground car park.

Vic Armstrong was the second unit director/stunt coordinator, an old friend and a man who'd been a great stunt performer in his own right – he wrote a book about it, modestly entitled *The True Adventures of the World's Greatest Stuntman*. We spent about three weeks filming in that underground car park.

At one point I was one of the baddies trying to break into the car, then we got electrocuted. I then jumped into a Mercedes and set off after Pierce Brosnan in the BMW. My job was to crash that Merc into another car after Bond releases a scattering of metal tyre-puncture stars from the BMW, which went well. All in a day's work. But the end of that car chase took us to Germany.

The car, remotely driven, has to go up a concrete car park's spiral ramp, up through the car park levels to the roof. Steve Street was still filming in the UK so I took another of the modified cars – we got through a lot – to Germany to get that sequence. We only had the one car and I had to drive it fast up and up, with concrete walls very near, and I really couldn't damage the BMW. It was disorientating and hairy, but it worked.

Which meant we were in good shape for the finale, where the BMW goes through the retaining wall on the roof, flies across the street many storeys up, and then smashes into the Avis office at ground level. Again, you'd probably think that was CGI, but we did it for real. We used a nitrogen cannon put together by Dave Bickers to fire the car out across the street. What a great way to end the sequence.

But we owed it all to a young man with hair down to his waist, who seemed about 12 years old. The BMW was so electronically sophisticated that every time our technical guys tried anything the car would sulk and go into go-slow mode. So BMW lent us the guy who'd designed the computer system. When we hit another glitch this young man would turn up, open the bonnet, plug in his laptop and fix the problem. We couldn't have made the film without him.

By *Die Another Day*, in 2002, the special effects team had really upped their game even further. This was Pierce Brosnan's fourth and final Bond film, and I was involved in the long car chase sequence on the frozen lake by the ice palace. The thing was, the Jaguar XKR and the Aston Martin V12 Vanquish just couldn't drive on ice.

The decision was taken to convert them from rear-wheel to four-wheel drive, and that meant ripping out the engines and replacing them with big-lump Ford V8s, naturally aspirated. These had Land Rover gearboxes and transfer cases, with a Ford Explorer front axle. Somehow the team got all that in place and working perfectly, delivering lots of power and torque to all four wheels.

They had plenty to do as we needed three of each of the cars, because of filming requirements and the risk of damage. I believe the bill just for the cars came to about a million pounds, but it was a phenomenal piece of engineering.

A small group of us went out to the main location in Iceland about a week before the main unit. The Icelandic authorities had given us permission to use a lagoon, which had had the inlet blocked so it was no longer tidal. There were icebergs in there and ice thickening all over it. But before we could get all the filming kit on it, the ice had to be 42cm thick.

For the advance team this restriction didn't apply, and we took the cars out on the ice every day to get the hang of driving them on such a difficult surface. We had three different sets of tyres with different length spikes, and found the intermediates worked best. We practiced accelerating, cornering, braking, everything, and got it pretty sorted, although braking was always a concern.

I thought we had it all under control until I watched a rough video of us driving on the ice at the end of one day. Behind my car you could clearly see a rippling wave forming as the ice flexed.

We'd known it would be hairy, which is why we drove in immersion suits. In the boots of the car were inflatable bags that would go off if we actually broke through the ice. The car would then hang nose down in the freezing water so that, in theory, we could get out. We didn't want to test that theory. We had the idea they were actually more worried about pollution than the stuntmen.

By the time the whole crew turned up we felt we had things under some sort of control, and could drift, do 360s and all the rest. Each morning, before dawn, we'd be up and heading to the lagoon. Each stunt driver (George Cottle and Ray De Haan) had his own skidoo, and we'd go out on the ice to recce conditions. Ray had a collision with an iceberg and I took over doubling Pierce for a couple of days, as well as driving the rocket sledge.

It was down to about minus 20 C at night, and always cold, but heading out on my skidoo in the dark let me experience some of the most magical dawns I've ever seen. The sun appearing behind the glacier was breathtakingly beautiful, truly memorable.

The sun shone and it didn't snow at all during the fortnight we were there. One old boy, a local, came up to tell us about how unusual the weather was being, which was perfect for filming. He smiled:

'God must love James Bond!'

13

In Fitness and in Health

'The self-discipline is applied by the pain.' Jim Dowdall

Working as a stunt performer is obviously a fairly demanding job. Working 18-hour days is pretty normal, as you'll have read about in earlier chapters. Up before dawn to work outside all day, then into the studio after dark until perhaps 10pm. Often in extreme cold and wet, for days and days on end. No chance to go home at weekends, just one day off to rest your battered body. God, I'm feeling sorry for myself.

There are two main requirements for keeping going under those circumstances – fitness and heath. I see a lot of stunt people really focused on their fitness, some of them going to the gym for hours every single day. They look sensational - but then you need to be if you're doing a long fight sequence, then another take, then another. The days can be incredibly draining.

People are more focused on the body beautiful now than when I was their age in the 1970s. Back then I was pretty fit and I was a natural athlete, but I've actually found life a bit too short to spend all my time weighing my food and working out.

When I was doing mostly stunts then I'd run every day - every day come rain or shine that I wasn't working. I lived in London then and I had my dog Dodger, so every day we'd go for a run round the Serpentine. He was one fit dog.

When I was a bit older, in my thirties, it changed because Dodger had died. To compensate for not having him around with me every day, I took out a membership at a posh gym in Hammersmith. I'd go and work out properly about three times a week. There were some very pretty people there, but it wasn't as much fun as running with Dodger.

At home I installed a pull-up bar halfway up the stairs. I had a rule. Every time I passed the bar, going up or down, I had to stop and do five chin-ups or pull-ups, no matter how often I used the stairs.

Most days I'd also hang upside-down from the bar to stretch out my battered spine.

I was fit but I wasn't fanatical about it, partly because I wasn't leaping off tall buildings much. Instead I was doing vehicle work with cars and motorbikes, or fire jobs. Most stunt work is in short bursts and I could still do a quick 100m, which was what was needed.

The big change for me came in my late thirties. By then I was doing more stunt co-ordinating, which isn't as physically demanding although the hours can be even longer. Up to that point I had the same waist and chest size as when I was a teenager, but co-ordinating meant I had less time to keep fit and that's when my body started to change a bit.

But then I bought a farm and there was a colossal amount of work to do on it, as well as walking the dogs I had then, so going to the gym didn't really seem necessary. Anyway, by the time I was in my fifties I was 'pointing the finger' more and more – getting stuntmen in to do the stunts I'd previously done myself.

But, like I say, I think there are two major elements to being a stuntman over time and the second, health, seems equally if not more important. And much of that is down to your diet. You might think stuntmen eat raw steak for breakfast and follow it up with half a dozen burgers for lunch, and maybe some do. There are certainly stunt people out there my age now who've started most days of their lives with a Full English breakfast. And now they're enormous because the older you get the longer it takes to get rid of the weight.

It helps that I never drank alcohol, which of course I have my parents to thank for, in a funny way. That just makes my life easier, except when it doesn't. I can't help myself when I'm in a social situation. I watch people drinking and there's always a point where I can see their attitude is going to change whether for the better or the worse because of the alcohol. Then the conversations become more distorted and it's time for me to leave. All my life when that happens I just want to be away from it because it's just got too many memories of my mother and father.

The main element is that I was never a junk food man. I've never eaten a Burger King or any of those, I don't know what a KFC tastes like. I don't have a sweet tooth, I'm not a pie man – I've always been like that. When I was at my mews apartment in London as a younger man there was a restaurant at the top of the mews that served the most fantastic salads at lunchtime. If I wasn't working that's where I went every day for a big vegetarian salad or perhaps a clean steak and salad.

I'm not a vegetarian or anything like that, but I was affected by working on *The Long Good Friday* with Bob Hoskins. There was this scene where some of us were hanging upside down in a meat locker. It was in a real slaughterhouse in Erith. We'd hang for ten minutes, then they'd come and slide a board in under our backs so that we could be lowered down to 45 degrees for a break without getting our feet untangled. It wasn't nice.

It was also 40 degrees in the summer and that slaughterhouse was dreadful. I never want to go to one again. The smell of frightened animals and blood and stuff as we hung there like slabs of meat ourselves – it was just frightful.

On a happier note, Bev and I got married in 1991 when I was 43 and she wasn't (she's 11 years younger than me). She was a Cambridge and London Business School graduate working in the City and hurling herself off mountains under a hang glider in her spare time. We met through a friend, Lucy Mcsweeny, who'd just become Ladies World Champion paraglider. We got married in Salehurst Church and I abseiled into the churchyard from a helicopter. Bev walked! Joanna Lumley (an old chum from *Avengers* days) came to read the lesson, and her lovely husband Stephen Barlow (the youngest master of the organ ever at Cambridge) came to play the church organ like I believe it's never been played before.

On a sadder note, it highlighted that I never really reconciled with my mother. Even when I was successful in terms of money, and I'd go and see her in her little house in Chelsea, which I'd bought really for her, she still let me know I was a bit of a disappointment. I mustn't be too hard on her, but she was a 'glass half empty' woman – and she drank a lot.

It was poignant really, because a few weeks before our wedding she was getting ready to go out and buy a hat for it. But she slipped on the steps of her house and banged her head pretty badly. She never really recovered from that. My mother missed the wedding and spent her last few months in various retirement homes.

But on the happiest of notes, our daughter Jordan arrived a couple of years later, being born on Friday the 13th but, as I was born on Halloween, we both thought that would be lucky. And it was.

We started our own organic vegetable patch on the farm and we just live it straight.

After we'd been together a couple of years, Bev gave up banking and venture capital and started to learn about Naturopathy, nutrition, massage and several other skills – none of which involved the dispensing of drugs. She has been a Naturopathic doctor now for over 20 years, seeing patients from all over the world. Among many, many things I've learned from her, she's helped me realise I'm wheat intolerant.

Recently, I spent a couple of days in Prague (getting a shotgun blast to the chest playing the part of an American gangster, and having to do dialogue with a New York accent…interesting), and then some days in Southern Europe. I ate a lot of bread and sandwiches for convenience, although I don't normally eat a lot of that stuff.

When I got back I could hardly move and one knee had completely ballooned up. A couple of days on a sensible diet without wheat and I was fine again. That's the advantage of living with a Naturopath. She recommends, and I absolutely take her advice.

That's what happens though when you don't have self-discipline.

However, the self-discipline is applied by the pain and the fact that you can't always get out of bed easily in the morning. I've actually started doing yoga because getting out of bed easily can be vastly improved by a couple of hours of said yoga.

⊙⊙⊙

The decades of stunts have taken their toll, of course, but there's no question it would have been much worse if I hadn't mostly moved over from stuntman to stunt co-ordinator. If you haven't made that move by the time you're 40 or 45, or shifted on to second unit director or something, you'll be in a world of pain. I was very lucky, and got my first stunt co-ordinator role early.

I'd actually only been a stunt man for about five or six years before I did my first co-ordinator job in 1978. At the time there was a bit of a fashion for Indian films to come over to the UK and shoot sequences here. I'd just finished working as a stuntman doubling Harrison Ford on *Hanover Street* when I got this gig to stunt co-ordinate on a film directed by, produced by and starring one Feroz Khan.

It was all a bit hand-to-mouth as we were being paid cash every day, but with just three days' filming to go it was clear we'd run out of money. It was Ramadan so the banks where the money was were shut for 30 days and we only had a couple of grand in the available account. I had about six stunt guys working with me, and we were behind on the money as it was. It all got a bit tense.

My buddy Nick Farnes, who was the English production manager for the shoot, got hold of the latest rushes (the rough film) and took it away and buried it all somewhere just in case there was a temptation to make a midnight flit – not that we thought it would come to that. Then the location manager told everyone he was betting on a horse in the 3.30 at Redcar. It was a 20/1 outsider but he told us with absolutely total confidence that the horse was going to come in. We went to talk to Mr Khan.

The upshot was that Feroz Khan's man put the final £2000 on this horse. I still remember us all squeezed into this little Winnebago with a tiny black and white television. I was standing in the doorway holding the aerial so we could get some sort of signal. It's the only horse race I've ever watched - and the bloody horse came in!

Khan's man appeared some time later that night with two suitcases full of £40,000 (there were no £50 notes in those days). We all got paid, we finished the film and we had the best 'end of picture' party I've ever been to. But it got better.

The film was called *Qurbani* (*The Sacrifice*), and instantly became a monster hit in India. It was the biggest hit of 1980 there, grossing the equivalent of $45m in today's money. Not bad for my first job as a stunt co-ordinator. And I got paid.

14

A YEAR IN THE LIFE

*'A year is a long time to live without the human contact
of loved ones, fresh air, and gravity, to name a few.'*
Astronaut Scott Kelly

So keeping on top of your game in a dangerous business means keeping fit and well. Same as it does for everyone – keep fit, eat healthy and you'll improve your odds no end. That means you'll have the stamina for the long haul, much as I had to find in 2000. I was in my early fifties then, I'd married about seven years before, and we'd had our daughter Jordan, who was still very young.

And that year I think I was home for about three and a half weeks all year.

It started with me getting the gig for a film I really wanted to work on: *Enemy at the Gates*, directed by Jean-Jacques Annaud. You have to go and pitch for the work as stunt co-ordinator. I'd met Jean-Jacques at a swanky London hotel and impressed on him my credentials in military films and my knowledge of the story of two snipers battling it out in the snowy wreckage of Stalingrad. I really wanted to work on this film and fortunately I got the job.

The two snipers were played by Jude Law and Ed Harris. I'd worked with Jude Law before, so I took him down to the Bisley Shooting Ground with a Nagant rifle with a telescopic sight – standard Russian issue for the period. When we got there, we stood looking out at the range, which had the targets a way off and just some scrubby, grassy ground between.

I asked him if he could see the sniper.

I'd got a mate of mine, who is a sniper, to dress up in his ghillie suit, along with his weapon. He was somewhere in front of us. Jude Law couldn't see him. He asked if he was 100 yards away. Nope, I said, closer. Fifty yards? Nope, closer. Thirty yards? Wrong again. He really studied the terrain but couldn't see him. I told my mate to stand up, which he did, about ten yards away. That just blew Jude Law away, and gave him a good idea of what we were trying to achieve.

This highly paid, famous actor then had 80 rounds to fire with the Nagant. I wanted to get him used to the real thing, used to aiming, firing and reloading as one continuous action. You have maybe half a second to see the fall of shot to see if you've got a hit before you work the bolt to get another round in. There's no point in having an empty rifle. There's quite a bump to the recoil, so he knew all about it after he'd fired all the rounds.

From there we headed to Berlin, where the action was taking place. There I also took Ed Harris out with a Mauser and 80 rounds to put him through the same drill on the ranges there. The German rifle kicks hard, and I kept telling him to keep back from the rear of the telescopic sights. It was very cold, January, and he was trying hard but on the 79th round out of 80 he got too close. The recoil smacked the rear of the sight into his eye socket and he needed three stitches in his eyebrow. He apologised, but in the early part of the film you can just make out a mark by his eye.

We were based in East Berlin in what had been the old Panzer barracks at Krampnitz. It was a weird place, like a time warp. It was only about 30km outside Berlin but neither the allies nor the Russians had realised it was there during the war so it hadn't been bombed. It had been home to a whole Panzer division's headquarters and, when the Russians moved in, they pretty much left it alone. They knocked the swastikas off the carvings of eagles on the roof and the fireplace, but that was about it.

An entire Russian tank division had been based there during the Cold War, about 250 tanks and 12,000 men, and now it was our playground. We'd be up before dawn having breakfast, then start shooting at first light until the day was dark, then we'd go inside and keep shooting until about 8pm. It was unbelievably cold the whole time.

I was very much on my own since I wasn't allowed any British stuntmen. Bapty's weren't supplying the weapons either, as that job was down to a Berlin company, Nefzer. I wasn't sure about them, then early on I noticed an MG 42 on a tripod they were setting up. The muzzle brake showed this wasn't a WWII German one, but a post-war Yugoslavian weapon – only an uber-geek like me would notice the difference. As I was also there in the role as military/historical adviser, I told the armourer I didn't want to see it on the set again. He understood – they had original gear – and from then on we got on like a house on fire. They had marvellous kit, and have since turned into good mates of mine.

Which was handy as the very first scene we shot was a monster, a huge charge across the square in Stalingrad. There's a big Russian population in Berlin and they wanted us to use Russians for Russians, so we'd have these casting sessions on Saturday mornings. Most of the guys turning up had been out drinking the night before and some were still drunk, although others made an effort to sober up. When we called them on the Monday morning to tell them if they'd got the job or not, half of them couldn't remember even turning up for the auditions.

The Russians in Stalingrad sometimes sent men into action with only one rifle between about three men – it was all they had. The idea was this wave rolled forward, and if a man was hit then you picked up his rifle and charged on. And I had about 150 or 200 of these Russians, with rifles and blanks, charging about, with explosions and all sorts. It wasn't relaxing.

In fact there were so many people that we had to modify our normal procedure. For an explosion going off, the special effects people rig the pot in the ground then set it off when the stuntman has just stepped over it. But there were so many people running around it would be easy to get it wrong, and firing it with a man right above it would not be pretty. So we got a load of pedals, which we painted in high-vis. The camera couldn't see them but the stuntmen could. We placed them, wired in to the pots, just on the far side of the pot so a charging man could run over the pot, step on the pedal and know the explosion was going to go off right behind him, giving him a split second to react to the blast.

Another big set-piece was the river crossing sequence, where we had about 250 Russians on the water in little boats. This was 20 years ago, and everyone was more gung-ho, but I made myself very unpopular by calling a halt. We had all these men on the water and the water was absolutely killingly cold. If anyone went in wearing their big Russian greatcoats and nobody noticed, they'd be lost in seconds. What to do?

I put a call in to a mate in England, Dave Shaw, who runs a film diving services company (and now runs the Underwater Stage at Pinewood). He was delighted to deal with an instant order for 250 flotation devices that would only inflate when they came in contact with the water. The production team were not impressed. Then they really started to hate me. Because I pointed out that if the men wore the devices under their greatcoats and they went into the water the rapid inflation would probably throttle them. So we had to move the buttons and sew Velcro on every single greatcoat. I could feel the love.

The battle scene was enormous and chaotic, or it appeared so, with explosions, bullet strikes and men shouting everywhere, but somehow we got away with it – I really do put some of that down to luck, as working on the water in crowded, freezing conditions was a serious challenge. Gerry Gavigan, the first assistant director (with whom I'd been doing Bond films for years), did a phenomenal job.

We were filming six days a week and I'd be on set by 6.30am in time for breakfast and then work. We'd go right on into the evening and, as stunt co-ordinator, I was doing quite a lot of standing around in freezing conditions, so for me one of the main questions was working out how many thermal layers and how much knickerage I could get on and still move.

I had my own very nice little flat in Berlin and there was no point in trying to fly home on a Sunday only to fly straight back again, so I stayed there for the whole filming, which was about four months. It was still freezing cold when I left, but at least I was then back home again with the family. For one week. Then I got on another plane to disembark in Kefalonia, Greece for *Captain Corelli's Mandolin*.

⊙ ⊙ ⊙

It was warm, it was beautiful, it was spring and I'd loved the book.

One of my first jobs was to teach Nicholas Cage how to ride the Moto Guzzi motorbike he'd be riding in the film. He could already ride and owned Harleys and stuff, but this had a different set-up so we fenced off a car park, got two of the bikes there, and I waited for the star to turn up.

We're in the middle of nowhere and then this convoy arrives, a fleet of Mercedes and people. A flunkey hops out to hold an umbrella over the star in case he gets too hot. I'm getting the idea. Then Nicholas Cage approaches and says:

'So, this motorcycle, it is like my Harley-Davidsons?'

Only he says it in a weird voice that makes him sound like an Italian Bronx hamburger salesman. He's in character and he won't come out of it. I teach him how to ride the bike and he gets it quickly, no problems at all, and then the convoy departs.

It was one of those things. Throughout filming we couldn't call him Nicholas or Mister Cage, it had to be Corelli or Capitano on or off the set. We were told not to make eye contact with him, all that stuff, and he turned up with his convoy more often than not. Then John Hurt arrived.

Naturally he got the whole treatment and they told him they'd send a limo to pick him up from his hotel every morning and so on. He told them not to bother. Every morning he'd turn up on a little rented 50cc twist-and-go scooter, have a roll-up and join me and the stunt boys for a cup of tea and a natter. A bit of a contrast.

The downside was we did a scene where one of my stunt boys got hurt. He was driving a truck that is attacked by a Stuka, so they had a whole load of squibs in the back as well as a bang. It was an open truck so there was no protection for driver Derek Lea. The special effects guys said the stuntman 'might get a bit warm'. I should have heard the alarm bells ringing.

I heard enough to make sure he wore some goggles. I wanted him to wear gloves but they wouldn't have it — it was 30 degrees. When the bang went off it just enveloped the whole truck in flames. Derek got burns on the backs of his arms and hands. Next time, I promised myself, I'd pay more attention when the special effects guys made some mild comment like that.

However the upside was that during filming Bev and Jordan came out for a couple of weeks and it was great to see my wife and daughter again. While there, Jordan learned how to swim like a dolphin and that was such a pleasure to watch.

At the end of another mammoth few months I flew home to be with the family again. At least I had time to settle in, this time for a week and a half, before heading up to Liverpool to shoot *51st State* with Samuel L Jackson in a kilt.

⊙⊙⊙

It was a very busy film for the stunt people as we had a lot of car chases, including a jump onto a barge. We used Kiante Elam, a black stuntman who had been doubling for Samuel L Jackson for about 20 years. It was a strange film and pretty action-packed for the team, but I still managed to find the odd day off. The boys tried to get Kiante to drink Guinness but he resisted right to the end!

The location gave me a chance to look around Liverpool. My grandfather, Harold Chaloner Dowdall, had been Lord Mayor of the city in 1908, and I got to see the Mayor's chair he'd have sat in. At one point we were filming right outside the town hall, where they were doing some roadworks. I looked into the hole and about eight inches down you could see tramlines, and I was thinking that my grandfather would have travelled on those trams. It was quite evocative.

However, most of the time I was busy organising ridiculous things on the film. That took another three and a half months, and then that was the year done. There was hardly any family time, but plenty of income time. In my fifties, it was a surprise to find I was on a bit of a roll, and I just wanted to keep it rolling. In this business, when you're hot you have to make the most of it. But I took a month off over Christmas.

15

THE PIANIST

*'This was a film that I could make with my eyes closed
because I had lived it and everything was still alive in me.' Roman Polanski*

As soon as the new year started I got a call to go and audition as stunt co-ordinator on a film about the Warsaw Uprising. I knew some of the stunt team since I'd worked with them for months the previous year, and I knew the true story of a pianist trying to survive in the ghetto in Warsaw. This was a subject I really wanted to work on, so I flew over to Berlin to meet the director, Roman Polanski.

He was a really legendary director in 2001, but he had a lot of Polish people on board at high levels so I didn't rate my chances. But having done *Enemy at the Gates* the previous year apparently counted for something, and I got the job.

I was aware that Polanski was emotionally involved with the project. He'd been asked by Steven Spielberg to direct *Schindler's List* but had turned it down, saying it was too personal for him to do.

As a boy, Polanski had been in the Krakow Ghetto, and seen terrible things, some of which he wanted to bring into *The Pianist*. His mother had died at Auschwitz and his father only just survived. This was a film with real meaning for Polanski, and the film is based on the autobiography by Wladyslaw Szpilman, an Auschwitz survivor, who had only died the year before, in 2000.

The film covers a long period, but the very first shot Polanski wanted to do was the start of the Warsaw Uprising, an absolutely huge scene. I'd noticed this before, like in *Enemy at the Gates*, you never get a chance to settle in and get to know how people work with a couple of easy scenes. It's always straight in at the deep end.

I had to juggle civilians, 30 German soldiers, two tanks, an overturned tram on fire and numerous shots and explosions. I was given one day to rehearse the whole battle scene. Except they wouldn't pay extra to have the tanks and tank crews there for the rehearsal. However, I knew most of the stuntmen, and the set was absolutely extraordinary.

They were busy rebuilding what had been East Berlin, ripping up all the cobbles and putting down tarmac. The art department found a site where the original old cobbles had been stashed and were given literally about a million of them to put down on the set. It made the set look brilliantly in period, although the cobbles weren't easy to run around on or fall over on.

It was winter and the light had gone by 3pm, so there was a bit of pressure, and we had a lot going on. There was a Panzerfaust that had to fire across the street into the Police Headquarters, and we had that running on a wire. Then there were Molotov cocktails, which were real ones, glass bottles full of fuel, that had to be thrown at stuntmen, who had accelerant on their clothing to burn fiercely.

It was all going on, but an added difficulty was that Polanksi wanted this all shot from Szpilman's point of view, from behind some curtains, so it all had to be done in one take as a master shot. No pressure then!

The next day, the first day of the shoot, I did my customary thing of pissing everyone off. Polanski was up behind the curtains, there were thousands of people about the place and there was a lot of tension. And I had to ask him for more rehearsal time. The issue was that I knew the tank drivers, who were solid, but they didn't know what was going on, and with lots of people about that's just too dangerous.

For a tank driver it's like looking through a letterbox - you really can't see much. But if you know three people are going to run across in front from left to right you know what to expect. And if you see two people cross, you stop because you might be about to run over the third. I explained all this to Polanski but in front of everyone he says:

'Oh so you want to stop the film? I cannot film because you want to stop the film?'

He was really sarcastic. I told him I needed 40 minutes for a run-through with the tank crews. I also pointed out that if we went for it and it didn't work it would take three hours to get everything reloaded and ready again. Very begrudgingly he gave me 40 minutes. We had one more run-through and then we had a go.

Fortunately we got it all in that one long shot. Polanski left the building, and came over and shook my hand. He said:

'English [his name for me], okay, now you tell me what you need and I'll do what you say.'

From then on we had a fantastic relationship and I loved working with him. Which meant I went out of my way – and out of my budget – to get a couple of shots that he wanted. How could I refuse? He actually remembered seeing both these things as a boy in the Krakow Ghetto.

He remembered a woman running down the street. She was innocent, just trying to get away from the fighting somewhere behind her. And a German soldier shot her between the shoulder blades. She fell to her knees and then just collapsed in that posture. She died, still kneeling, and she was there for about two days because everyone was too scared to go and move her.

I found a local stunt lady and dressed her up and made sure she had some solid pads for her knees because those cobbles were hard. We rehearsed it and got that shot as he remembered it, and then moved on to the second. He remembered a man being deliberately run over by a truck, over his legs, so we set that up too. You need to dig a hole where the man's legs can hide while the truck runs over the dummy legs that are stretched out on the cobbles, attached to the man.

I know people have different views on Roman Polanski but he made an amazing film that clearly mattered a great deal to him and to others who endured what he'd endured as a young boy. And he was pretty amazing. He was approaching 70 at that point but he was running around everywhere like a kid. He kept wanting to show the stuntmen how he wanted them to fall or whatever, so I ended up running around after him with a judo mat so at least he wouldn't hurt himself too much. At one point I had to physically stop him trying to climb a drainpipe to demonstrate what he wanted to the stuntman. That was our job, but the energy of the man was extraordinary.

I was probably only on set for two or three weeks but I was very sad to leave that film. I just loved the whole experience, which I found so moving and poignant that I actually shed a little tear when I left.

16

GAGS

'You can dab on the embrocation with £50 notes.' Jim Dowdall

In the business a stunt is known as a 'gag'. Only sometimes it's hard to tell who the joke is on. With technology advancing at a ferocious rate, it's a business that is constantly evolving, but there are some gags that you could say were the bread and butter of stunt work.

It's as easy as falling through a window. Occasionally, you have to smash through real toughened glass, but most times you'll be going through what we call toffee glass. It looks like the real thing but won't cut you into pieces.

However, about 30 years ago I was doing a stunt in Denmark and I had to fall through a glass skylight. Because the toffee glass was horizontal rather than vertical, it had to be thicker, but that wasn't a problem. The set builders realised it was heavier so they made slightly stronger wooden battens to hold it in place. That didn't seem to be a problem either. Then I had a fall – I've had many.

I went through the glass and landed safely on the bed of wooden boxes I'd placed underneath. At that point I realised one of the wooden battens had smashed and gone straight through my thigh, from one side and out the other. I'd never have thought that might happen. It was like being hit by an arrow – which, as I mentioned earlier, I'd also experienced.

However, there are some jobs where for some reason you can't use toffee glass, and you have to smash through proper toughened glass panes. That's a much bigger deal. The way to get through those is to put a small detonator in the corner of the glass. I then charge the glass with a button to the detonator in my hand. When I'm about a foot away I press the button and that starts the breaking, crazing process so that it's just starting to break as I smash into it.

Obviously timing is critical and I'd only give the button to a special effects guy if I was totally confident he was on the case. I did once have a detonator fail to go off and I hit the glass and bounced back, virtually knocking myself out. I found out toughened glass is tough.

But when it works it looks spectacular. The downside is that you know you're going to land in the broken glass and you always get cuts and things. Gloves are one answer. Some years ago I bought some ladies gloves in a rather grand hosiery department. They're flesh-coloured and I bought about half a dozen pairs. Heaven knows what the lady serving thought I was buying them for, and she probably wouldn't have believed me if I'd told her.

Those gloves are just one of the thousand ways a stuntman learns through experience. But when you're a rookie it's all too easy to simply go with what other people tell you. As I said in Chapter 6, where I ended up on a freezing beach with just rotten old dead fish to keep me warm, at first you're not sure of what you can do, and you can get pushed around.

You have to work out how the stunt can best be done so that it balances the effect the director wants with the practicalities of actually getting it done without major risk to life and limb. One of my very first jobs as a stuntman was a perfect illustration. And we'll pass over the fact that I was wearing a one-piece silver outfit complete with antennae on my head.

I was Marvik and he was from Mars. He was there to teach kids in a safety film that farmyards are not a safe place to play – that tells you how long ago it was. So Marvik, complete with glitter, and looking like a slightly slimmer Teletubby, comes down from Mars and is somewhat bemused by all the agricultural equipment around the place. I had to fall off a tractor, between it and the trailer behind to show how dangerous it all was, but the last gag involved messing about in a grain silo.

Anyone who's seen the grain silo shoot-out in *Witness* with Harrison Ford knows that a silo with grain pouring in from the top is a seriously dangerous place to be. Marvik didn't know this and he dropped in. The silo was already about half full of grain and the director told me to simply hang around there and they'd pour tons of grain in from the top. If I kept my hands above my head, when they couldn't see my hands they'd stop pouring and then I could just wave and pull myself up. I was new to the game, but if I'd done what they asked I'd have been dead.

Because the grain is like quicksand. There's nothing to get a purchase on and you simply sink until you're smothered with not just the grain but also the dust. So the only way forward I could see was to drain the silo until it was about quarter full and I could then crouch down in the grain with my feet on the solid base. After the grain was added I could then stand up and all would be well. But they couldn't understand why I was holding things up and making trouble.

However, I stuck to my guns and they had to empty a lot of grain out and then we shot it. It was still spooky with all that grain falling, and I kept my hands above my head until I couldn't feel any air on them. I held my breath for another few seconds and then managed to force myself upright. They weren't happy. They'd wanted me to stay under for longer.

But actually they'd got the shot they needed and I lived to fight another day — both goals had been achieved. To achieve that I'd had to not only point out the problem but also provide the solution and stick with that solution. Live and learn.

Sadly, on the farm where this was shot, about ten years later a boy really did get killed by falling into a silo filled with grain.

But messing about in a silo of grain doesn't even look like a stunt to most people. Ask them what a stuntman does and they'll think of explosions, flames, bodies flying around. And key to so many of those stunts is the pot, something I've mentioned before.

The pot is made of steel and has an explosive charge at the bottom. Then you add Fuller's Earth, bits of burnt cork and other stuff. That's right, you're getting blown up by the stuff you add to your cat litter tray. Then the pot is buried in the ground, and wired up to a switch that will set the explosion off. Usually a technician will hit the switch just as the stuntman reaches the far side of the pot. The stuntman then reacts by hurling himself forward, arms windmilling, dropping weapons and kit, as the explosion goes off right behind him.

Sometimes we place pedals just beyond the pot so the stuntman can tread on it and set it off himself — useful when there are a lot of people running around, like in *Enemy at the Gates*. The other advantage of this is that the stuntman knows to the millisecond when it's going to go bang, and can react at once — occasionally there's a slight delay between the explosion and the stuntman realising it's gone off and reacting.

It's a tried and tested system and it's never worth cutting corners – again, as in life. So what happens when you do cut corners? When we were working on *Force 10 from Navarone*, in Yugoslavia (as it was then) in the middle of winter, the ground was absolutely frozen, so digging down to put the pots in was a trial. The special effects guy figured with the ground so hard he didn't need the pots at all, so he just dug a pit and piled everything in.

Terry Walsh did a gag with one of those, and a stone came up with the Fuller's Earth and buried itself in his bum. I was shooting the same stunt the next night and a stone came up and cut my eyebrow open – if I'd have been looking down it would have caught me right in the eye. The special effects guy started digging pits for the pots.

Depending on the amount of explosive and stuff in the pot, you can get quite a substantial explosion, so it really does look like a shell has just landed. There's a big cloud of flame, smoke and debris, but at least it's behind you and you're rapidly moving away from it. A fire job is different.

Being set on fire isn't everyone's cup of tea, not even for some on the Stunt Register, but I have to say I'm really happy with fire. I'm confident of my kit and a burn job is about self-confidence not bravery. I know I can do it.

It's also about everyone knowing exactly what is going to happen, so we rehearse and rehearse, naturally without any flames. One of the elements that can help is a wind machine. When you're on fire, it's better to run into the wind, otherwise flames can get into your face and then into your mouth and nose when you breathe in.

When we're ready I go and get dressed. I start with fireproof underwear, which is soaked in a barrier gel. I have to say that's not a great start because the barrier gel has to be really cold so it goes on straight from the fridge. Then a one-piece Nomex suit goes on, a bit like Formula One drivers wear, then special silver foil over the known hotspots like legs and back. Then over that goes the outfit I'll be wearing for the part. My head and hands are then coated in a barrier gel, and then I'm ready, unless it's a 'full burn'.

For a full burn I'll have a silicone mask with nose holes in it. The eyeholes are covered by two bits of oven glass. I then get into position and check everyone I need is there – this is a team effort. There will be a fireman, a proper paramedic with defibrillator and all the gear, and another stuntman whom I trust standing exactly where I'm going to finish my scene. He's got a CO_2 canister.

Everyone then gets ready and double-checks everything. Then we get the command to go. A technician daubs some gloopy accelerant over the clothes with a spatula. From that moment we have exactly 60 seconds to get the stunt done before the accelerant begins to go 'off' and lose its flammable properties. Someone will then approach me with a blowtorch. When he hears 'Action' he sets me on fire.

I now have 15 to 20 seconds to get the scene done before the flames start to heat through all the protective layers. I'm usually running, waving my arms, and looking in agony, but I have to say when I'm doing a fire job my pulse isn't that raised. I have total confidence in my kit, it's the best available.

I always make sure I'm running into the wind, and I then throw myself down in front of the stuntman with the CO_2 canister and he whooshes me down until all the flames are out. That's when I check to see if I've got burned. I've never been badly burned, just some scorching and a bit of blistering – but you can dab on the embrocation with £50 notes.

The last fire job I remember was probably about 18 months ago, so you can keep doing them. I've done them because I'm totally confident doing them and they pay well. Simple. Also it's one of those situations where a great deal of the whole stunt is under my control. That helps with the self-confidence, to know you've got it all covered off.

Other stunts you're not so in control – the reality is that nobody is. One example would be a gag I performed on *Indiana Jones and the Last Crusade*. You might remember there's a huge boat chase through the waterways of Venice. Harrison Ford's speedboat hurtles between two huge ships which are slowly edging together. The bad guys – that's me – try to follow. Indy pops out the front like a cork from a bottle but the bad guys get crushed and blow up, with a wall of flames and debris, and one dying villain, hurtling into view.

They achieved this by placing the camera angle almost side on so you can't see that the two ships aren't really touching. Between them they built a raft. On this raft they set a hinged steel plate called an air ram, fired by a high-powered nitrogen canister. There were also huge pots of explosive and cork just under the deck where the ram sat. I had to run down the raft and onto the steel plate. As I ran onto it, a solenoid would trigger the nitrogen and this would fire the explosive and the air ram simultaneously, hurtling the steel plate up from flat to almost vertical. That would propel me up and forward and into the view of the camera.

Or, if anything went slightly wrong, it would catapult me directly upwards to fall back on the edge of the thick steel plate. Or, if I wasn't running right, it would break my kneecaps. A couple of possibilities there.

But it all worked out fine. I hit the plate right and got slammed forward. At the same time all the pots went off and I windmilled through the air surrounded by flames and burning debris. But, fortunately for me, before I could get burned, I landed in the freezing, filthy water so that put out any flames. A boat came and fished me out and it was time for tea and medals.

17

CAR-CRASH TV

'It buys a few bruises.' Jim Dowdall

If you think of the staples that make up action films then explosions are definitely one, and another is the car chase. Cars speeding, drifting and of course crashing. Getting a car moving fast to turn over isn't that hard and there are a couple of tried and tested ways of doing it. Getting a slow-moving vehicle to roll is more of a challenge.

This was a problem I encountered while working on *The English Patient*. We'd gone out to Tunisia to film a sequence where a rebuilt but genuine Model A Ford truck has to teeter on the edge of a sand dune and then roll sideways down the slope. I knew we needed to fit a rollcage but couldn't for the life of me work out how the Ford was going to do anything other than flop onto its side in the sand. How could it roll down the slope?

Fortunately a pair of Dave Bickers' boys came to the rescue, once again. Dick and Lou were a legend in the film business. They'd been working together for about 35 years and simply knew everything. We started the film at Cinecitta Studios in Rome, and Dick and Lou were filming *Daylight* (with Sylvester Stallone) very close to us and were prepping the vehicles for that, but I caught them in their valuable lunch hour. I explained the problem. They nodded, paused for thought and Dick said 'Peanut'. They both nodded. I nodded. I had no idea what they were talking about.

Bless them, they were insanely busy but they made me a steel cage to be bolted in the back of the Model A. Inside the cage was something that looked like a slice out of a swiss roll, about two-foot diameter. It was made of solid lead and weighed about half a ton. This was Peanut.

I had no idea if this would work, but we got out to Tunisia and got the truck jacked up at the point of balance on the top of this sand dune and all the cameras were ready. We had to have someone in the truck in case it landed on its wheels and rolled into people, but the rollcage would keep them safe. Fingers crossed, it was time to see if Peanut could do its thing. The truck went over.

It was obvious we'd have one take at this before the truck was damaged, but it worked fantastically. As the truck went over, Peanut rolled to one side of the cage and the weight was enough to keep the Ford rolling as Peanut rolled along and round. The only downside was the sound man complaining that all he could hear was this thundering 'clunk, clunk, clunk' as Peanut smashed into the cage, but that was a small detail for post production.

When my daughter was younger I had some mechanical problem with a vehicle I was working on at home and wondered out loud how to fix it.

'We need Dickenlou', she said. She'd heard the names so often she assumed it was one person. She was right.

◉◉◉

If I'm doing a car crash job then the car gets a Bickers bespoke rollcage. I worked with Dave Bickers for years and years, but he died a few years ago and I really miss him. However, his son Paul has taken over the business and he and his team are the only people I'll use to make a rollcage. I know I'll be safe with them. Every cage is made to fit the particular car so you see as little as possible of it, but it's going to do its job.

Back in the day you could use some old MoT write-off if it was just going to get rolled through the scenery, but not now. I remember driving one old scrapper years ago and the rollcage punched right through the rotten floor, pinning my hand to the roof of the car. But we don't do that any more. The base car has to be a proper roadworthy vehicle with a valid MoT. We'll remove the fuel tank, fit a roll cage and make sure the battery is replaced with a dry-cell battery and boxed in with an external isolator.

Again, all of this helps with the self-confidence that you can do the stunt and you're going to be okay. I've never broken anything doing car crashes, but preparation and the right kit are both paramount. If the Bickers boys have built the cage and I've got the Corbeau-type racing seat and five-point harness tightened up and the helmet is on right, then I *should* be fine. I always wear long hockey pads, which go from my toes to my knees, since pedals and bits of bulkhead can crush into you.

And lately I've had the luxury of a HANS device, like F1 drivers use, which fits to the helmet and stops whiplash. Even so, you know you're going to get banged about and come out of it a bit blitzed, but there is a financial compensation. It buys a few bruises.

And, again, it's one of those gags where you have a certain amount of control, which is backed up in my case by decades of experience of doing them. I've just about stopped doing car stunts, but was happily doing them well into my late sixties. It's a skill I learned a long time ago. Here's how a car crash works.

There are two main ways of turning a car over: the pipe ramp and the cannon. The pipe ramp is what it says on the tin, it's a ramp made with a solid roughly 75mm pipe mounted at an approximate 45 degree angle on a frame which is then bolted into the road. It's built just to one side, so the car approaches on the road and hits it so one side of the suspension rides up the angled pipe ramp, which is covered in grease.

The car is now angled up one side and at the end of the pipework is a 'kicker' which is a bit of pipe that's angled up further, for the final kick to punch the front of the car into the air and help make it roll. You can adjust the angle on the kicker depending on how many rolls you want the car to do and dependant on the speed of hitting the ramp. The pipe ramp works well, so long as the stuntman ensures he's driving up the ramp with the suspension on the pipe not the tyres That can be quite tricky if you're going fast, but that's the job you have to do.

The cannon is again pretty much what it sounds like. Only the cannon is in the passenger seat beside you, pointing down through the floor at the ground. Inside the cannon is an aluminium piston and that's powered by a tank of nitrogen which is boxed securely in the rear of the car. So you drive the car down to the point where you need to be in the road, start a handbrake turn, and hit the button for the cannon.

That fires the piston down into the ground and that rolls the car. You can fine-tune reasonably precisely how many rolls you're going to do by making decisions on car speed and the amount of nitrogen pressure in the cannon. That's where experience comes in, balancing those two. I'll have a reasonable idea of how far the car is going to go and how many rolls it will do, based on the road surface, speed, the type of car and the pressure in the cannon to within about 100psi. And you get paid according to the pressure of the gas and the speed of the car – more pressure and speed equals more fee!

I've rolled a lot of cars, but my pulse is still high for these things. It's not so much the perceived risk, since I'm in a car that has had thousands of pounds spent on it and it's been put together by people I trust implicitly. And that's the worry. There's been a lot of money spent and there have been lots of rehearsals and there's always a lot riding on it. Is the car going to end up where I want it to finish? You want that end point to be as near the camera as possible, but you have to do it without destroying the camera. That's why there are nerves - there's a lot invested in the point where you press the button.

As ever, you're trying to balance contradictory demands. The directors want the chariot race from *Ben Hur* for five bob. They want spectacular, I want to minimise the risk, and sometimes that means curbing their natural ignorance of what they're asking for.

And, once again, this is a team effort. As with a fire job, I'll want a fireman, a paramedic and also another stuntman to cut me out if necessary. Other stuntmen have broken their necks being dropped out of their harness if upside down. They'd done the stunt, and were in fine working order, and then they get a broken neck through lack of knowledge and experience. The aim is always to minimise unnecessary risk. It's a good aim for everyday life for everyone, not just stunt performers.

Budget is an issue. On a blockbuster like *Mission:Impossible* they can just throw money at it. They'll have three or four cars and do a take on each car and then decide which one they like the best after reviewing the film. With all these stunts you only get one take per car, after that the car's wrecked. That's quite a bit of pressure.

Of course two wheels are easier to crash – people manage it all on their own all the time. I've laid down a lot of bikes, but a motorcycle and sidecar is a different proposition because of the way the whole thing is asymmetrically balanced. I mentioned in Chapter 3 about *The Dirty Dozen: Next Mission* with Lee Marvin. One of the things I had to do was flip over a motorcycle and sidecar when we get 'hit' by an explosion. It's not that difficult actually.

To start with we had to load the front of the sidecar with heavy, wet sandbags to make it front heavy. The mechanics then welded a tyre iron to the bottom of the front of the sidecar about two inches off the ground. When I got to the appointed spot at speed, I wrenched the handlebars over, the tyre iron dug into the ground and the whole outfit flipped over, propelling me off the bike and into a hedge. The dodgy thing about this gag is that, if your foot gets stuck between the bike and the sidecar, you go over and finish up wearing the whole thing on top of you. Not recommended.

18

CAMELS AND DUKWs

'Where a Man Belongs.' 1980s Camel Cigarettes advert

I've had four-wheel drive vehicles since I had a driving licence. My Austin Champ was followed by my 1942 Jeep and, after that, I drove only Range Rovers for 32 years before switching to Subaru. I was a very early member of The All Wheel Drive Club in the 1960s and used to compete in the Jeep by taking off the windscreen, and removing the jerrycan and the bonnet. I'd then get the Jeep plastered in mud, replace the taken off bits at the end of the event, and go to work in it the next day.

In 1992 I was asked to drive a film crew who were going to cover the Camel Trophy expedition in Brazil and Guyana. This was to be serious four-wheel driving in the jungle with expedition-prepared Land Rover Defenders and early Discoverys. The Camel Trophy was an annual competitive event held between international crews in usually remote and difficult terrain. The name refers to the sponsor of the time, Camel Cigarettes, rather than the mode of transport.

After an acclimatisation period deep in the jungle for a week before the start of the expedition, we tried river crossings and making jungle bridges. The heat and the insects were interesting to say the least. Our first assistant director, Barry Wasserman, had never slept under canvas before and was a bit nervous. He got some awful stomach bug on day two and vomited and shat his way through the next few days until we could drive him back and put him on a plane home. I used to take him down to a river in the morning, strip him off and pour buckets of water over him and wash his hair to get rid of all the previous night's debris. It was a bit like a morning at an exclusive spa resort.

We started the expedition in Manaus, where there is the wooden opera house erected in the 19th Century which featured in the film *Fitzcarraldo*. There were about 40 vehicles carrying teams from different countries who'd fought their way over the previous year in various heats to represent their country.

We got deeper and deeper into the jungle and various mishaps befell the crews, like crashing into a hornets' nest, which rolled into one of the Discoverys and badly stung everyone aboard.

We had to cover just over a mile one night in mud that was up to a metre deep. It meant pulling out the winch cable to its full extent, attaching it to a tree and winching it in and then repeating the process. It took all night in the pissing rain to cover that mile. We wore head torches, which illuminated the huge ruts made by four-tonners. There were cayman (small alligator types) living in the ruts and you had to walk ahead with a broomstick to keep them moving. Quite unnerving, seeing the water disturbed in front of you as the reptile shot off a bit further along the rut!

We actually had to drive down some rivers, which we used like a road. We had to leave the windows open in case the vehicle dropped into a hole and you might have to swim out through the window. Water in the electric windows meant that for hours after the immersion, the windows would raise and lower indiscriminately, which was slightly alarming.

We arrived in Georgetown, Guyana after 18 days in the jungle, during which I'd managed to drop our Defender on its side twice due to the colossal weight of all the camera equipment we carried making it a bit top heavy. That was marginally embarrassing and a serious amount of piss taking took place until one of the Camel Trophy drivers did the same thing with our Defender and could thus see the problem! We took the piss out of him even more of course.

It was an extraordinary trip which cemented some friendships for life and taught me even more about four-wheel driving in the most challenging conditions.

By this time I was the part owner of a WWII amphibious DUKW, a large US army truck which had a waterproof hull and a propeller on the rear. The 50th anniversary of D-Day (the Allied invasion of France in 1944) was imminent so we got together with some other DUKW owners and decided we'd 'swim' the English Channel in our 50+ year old vehicles. It took us eight hours at a hull speed of about four knots but we all reached France safely. We drove up the beach at Wissant and avoided any Customs purely accidentally, as we'd been aiming for the hovercraft port at Calais but got swept further south by the current.

I had my 1942 Harley-Davidson on the rear deck and we lowered that down on the beach, and I then 'policed' the DUKWs all the way down to Normandy. We met so many extraordinary veterans, including an old DUKW driver who'd driven one up the beach at Arromanches at about 11am on the morning of D-Day. His mate's DUKW just behind him had received a direct hit, killing the crew. He hadn't seen a DUKW since he was demobbed so we got him and his wife in the front and took them out for a trip around the Mulberry Harbour remains. He was absolutely made up with that and I then let him drive the DUKW out to sea on his own. He hadn't forgotten a thing and did it beautifully. One of the great things about owning and running old military vehicles!

19

CARS – IN FRONT AND BEHIND THE CAMERA

'The closer you are to death, the more alive you feel.' James Hunt, Rush

Rolls-Royce and Morgan – what do they have in common? Out of all the main British, European and Japanese car manufacturers, they're the only two I haven't driven for. With over 400 car commercials in the can, that's a lot of footage – and a lot of bangs.

It must be said that modern car ads are considerably tamer than they used to be. I understand the reasons, but back in the day they were seriously eye-catching. Watch some old car commercials and they can look exciting and fun, and they were meant to be. But we weren't just playing around, there was a serious purpose.

I once did a commercial for Mazda, for its 626. It was such a fantastic commercial for Mazda – and for me – because it showed and showed and got results in the showroom. I got paid a lot for it, but actually that equated to about the unit cost of two cars, and I think it increased their showroom sales by something like 27%, directly attributable to that commercial.

It was based on the idea that the 626 only had two main rivals, the Porsche 928 and a Mercedes 190. In the commercial, these two rivals are driving along and the 626 comes up behind them and simply drives over the pair of them before accelerating away. It looked amazing and we did it for real.

We started by taking the engine out of the Porsche and bolting the Mercedes to the Porsche. That way they were side by side and the Mercedes was the donkey driving both of them. We then put rollcages in both cars so the roofs wouldn't collapse when I drove over in the Mazda. The bonnets were also reinforced, because I didn't want those collapsing either.

At the rear we put a pair of narrow ramps that were towed behind both cars, both of them just with nylon scrapers on the road so they wouldn't spark. They were pretty narrow to stay out of sight, so as I approached in the Mazda I had to line up very precisely so the front wheels drove up the ramps.

I then kept the power on as the front-wheel drive Mazda drove up the rear of both cars and onto the roofs. As the front wheels started down the windscreens I had to accelerate hard so that I would clear the bonnets and hit the ground ahead, otherwise I'd have nosedived into the road right in front of them and they'd have piled into me. That was a spectacular ad.

Spectacular but, in its way, a fairly straightforward one from my perspective. Something like the first Ford Mondeo commercial was technically more challenging. It was shot in Israel, out in the desert, and we built something like a third of a mile of single-track rail. This was because the idea was that you saw two elements of the car, one skeletal, the other less so, coming towards you. With some clever camera work the two then morphed together.

But for that to happen the two car elements had to be driven at very precise speeds so they could be morphed together. I was sat in the back of the skeletal car, dressed in a silver suit so I wouldn't show up. For space, I had to sit sideways to the direction of travel, looking once again at a tiny television monitor. It was hot, it was disorientating given the car was moving at 90 degrees to where I was facing, and my eyes were glued to the digital speedometer.

I had to drive the car, through fairly crude controls, at a speed that needed to be within 0.4mph. Then do the same thing with the other car. It worked. Then I had to get back in the skeletal car and drive it round the mountain passes. Sitting sideways watching a tiny screen of the road ahead while I was sat facing the huge drops beside the road certainly kept me concentrating.

I did a commercial for pretty much the final Ford Granada a year later. The gag for me was pretty straightforward: I had to drive the car up the upper deck of a car transporter and launch it towards the horizon. The upper deck is a fair way up and with speed I reckoned I'd launch into the air for quite a distance. But how far exactly?

That was the thing, there were no computer simulations, I had to work out where I was going to land. And that mattered because I needed my box bed to be in the right place. It was an impressive thing, four layers of cardboard boxes separated by sheets of plywood and covered in blue tarpaulins. The idea was that the car would smash through each layer of boxes and the sheets of ply would help it sink in managed, level stages, like a lift going down. That was the idea.

But of course it wouldn't be a lot of good if it was too near or too far. Standing on the top of the transporter, I made the call and we placed it where I reckoned I'd land. Time to buckle up.

The launch went well. And the landing went well. I landed exactly where I thought I would and the car came down beautifully level. In fact I got out to inspect the damage to the car. I'd cracked the rear numberplate, that was it. Another's day's work.

A few years ago, the first air bags were starting to be fitted in cars and Volvo were right there in the vanguard. I was asked to test the airbag on the new Volvo 340 for a TV commercial. I duly appeared at the studio, where Bickers had rigged a truck sideways on to the car route and placed a five-ton concrete block against the rear wheels. The Volvo people told me I had to hit the 'immovable' object at 27mph or more to initiate the air bag. There was a high-speed camera recording my face actually coming into the airbag. I was determined that, whatever happened, I wasn't going to wreck their car and not have the airbag go off, so I really went for it.

I had naively assumed it must work on compressed air as nobody had said different. When the car impacted, the air bag deployed (using a small explosive charge) and my face impacted the bag. However, it's quite a whack, and I was unconscious for a few seconds before I woke up to a smell of burning and the guys leaning in to switch off the motor, which was still running at full revs. I had abrasion marks on my nose, chin, cheekbones and eye sockets from the Kevlar airbag impact. The man from Volvo then said to me in a very Swedish accent: 'You should have put Vaseline on your face and you would have avoided that.' Thanks pal!

It worked well on the high-speed camera as I didn't know what was coming. We did it a second time and I was clearly anticipating the impact by screwing up my eyes in expectation, so that didn't work so well. But I did have the Vaseline. Such is the life of a genuine crash test dummy.

◉◉◉

Gags like that gave me steady work over the years and no bad injuries, but the move to stunt co-ordinator moved me back behind the camera. Usually that meant less risk. Usually. Working on the film *Rush,* though, certainly got the tension rising again.

With my experience I was given the job of being in control of the camera pursuit car, a specially adapted Mitsubishi Evo VIII, complete with camera pods front and rear. That was one fast car, and for most jobs it would probably count as overkill. But we were trying to keep up with historic Formula One cars. And it was hairy!

The car was set up all wrong, with 120kg of camera gear and pods front and rear, plus a camera operator inside, so you had a lot of contradictory demands. It had monstrous understeer and we were always fiddling with tyre pressures and stuff. And if I had two crewmen inside then I had to remember that it would handle differently on lefts compared to rights.

We were shooting at the Nurburgring, and that's a challenging circuit in its own right. I know the track fairly well but after a few corners, with all the demands from the crew, every corner started to look the same. I'd walked much of the sections we were using, but it still just blurred after a few corners.

And then there was the matter of millions of pounds' worth of classic racing cars, either in front or behind. When they were in front it was a case of trying to keep up since even old F1 cars are seriously fast. The problem was that the drivers didn't have experience of filming so they didn't know to look in their mirrors enough. I was flat out but still couldn't get up with them and was falling behind.

And I then had the added responsibility of Ron Howard, the director, sometimes sitting in the passenger seat saying 'go faster' while I countered with 'Guvnor, you're one of the top directors in the world and if I prang this thing and hurt you or the guys in the back, I couldn't live with myself – on top of the fact that I'd probably be out of work for ever.'

Then I'd get on the radio asking the drivers to ease up just a bit. Then of course, since they hadn't got brake lights, it was hard to see that they'd slowed quite hard and suddenly I was barrelling into the back of them. It was really quite stressful.

But the sound when you were behind them, particularly when we had the real cars, like the six-wheel Tyrrell, was phenomenal. When we shot the final Japanese GP, which was shot in England, we were on the grid at the start and they take off and you're trying to find a slot between them and we're sliding all over the track in the wet – it was absolutely deafening and so exciting.

Could doing stunts with cars get any wilder or more exciting? Well yes! About six years ago, I had to drive a new Jaguar car on two cables 70ft up crossing the Thames. It was a bit nervy, but all done because I had confidence in the riggers – and a Guinness World Record at the end of it I believe. And on that bombshell …

20

IN TOP GEAR

'Oh no, that's not what we wanted.
We wanted a massive fail.' Top Gear *producers*

When I've got a fire job or a near miss between a car and a truck or something like that coming up, it can prey on my mind for a day or two beforehand. But I can honestly say I've never literally lost a night's sleep over it. But I did miss an entire night's sleep when I was looking after the three boys on *Top Gear*. The cause was a sequence where the three were driving a variety of HGV trucks into a variety of obstacles. And Jeremy Clarkson was going to drive a truck through a brick wall.

We'd constructed the wall carefully, with a loose mortar mix between the bricks. But it was still a ton and a half of bricks. It was a slab-fronted truck so we'd strengthened the cab and put mesh over the windscreen, but I wasn't happy. I watched the rehearsals and tried to talk to Jeremy but he said it would be fine. About 3pm, with the shoot happening in the morning, I made a decision.

I got the Bickers boys to fix yet more strengthening to the cab by adding more RSJs and stuff, and doubling the mesh on the windscreen. I drilled holes in the back of the mortar in the wall. But he was still going to hit it at 40 or 50mph. That night I just could not sleep, worrying that we hadn't done enough. Eventually morning came.

I told Jeremy to make sure that whatever he did he wasn't to hold the steering wheel tight, but was to just keep his hands loosely on the rim. I told him he needed to wear a neck brace but he turned that down for how it would look in the shots. I made him put on armoured shin pads and he told me to stop fussing. I didn't think anyone else was taking this seriously enough. I bet him £20 he was going to 'feel it'.

Then he did the stunt. Give him points, he never lifted off the accelerator! It was one hell of a bang, and when we got to him we saw that the whole steering box had been ripped off the chassis. I was the first person to the cab door with the camera crew right behind, looking for that reaction shot. When I opened the door I waved them back for a minute.

Jeremy was totally socked. He'd taken a big hit. He'd held on to the steering wheel tight. The spinning steering wheel chipped a bone or something in his hand. He'd whacked his foot very badly on the pedals – at least he'd been wearing shin pads. He didn't know what day of the week it was for a while. He looked like he needed some sleep. I knew how he felt.

That was a busy bit of filming, since the other two were expected to crash trucks as well. Richard Hammond was to drive his through a Portakabin, which involved building a ramp and then gutting the Portakabin to weaken it, but not so much that it collapsed before Richard arrived in his seven-tonner. That went fine, but then they wanted to get James May to hit one of those standalone swimming pools. 'It'll be spectacular' they said. I agreed – it would be spectacular but for all the wrong reasons.

You have to remember that a cubic metre of water weighs one tonne. And that swimming pool contained many, many cubic metres. It was a flat-fronted truck and when it hit the side of the pool it would be like hitting concrete. It would stop absolutely dead. The team didn't consult with James on this but they just couldn't see that there was any sort of problem, and even turned down my suggestion of fitting a cow-catcher on the front to pierce the pool wall so it wouldn't be one flat surface hitting another. Time to lose sleep again.

Fortunately we reached a compromise, lost the pool idea and instead had loads and loads of plastic water containers, about 14 yards of them on different level shelves, for James to impact. Even then I wasn't happy with the weight and mass. So I went through them and drilled holes in the ones that would be directly in the eyeline of the windscreen so that he'd only ever be hitting empty containers at windscreen height. Again, it worked out fine in the end, but the crew's inability to understand how dangerous their ideas were was always a worry.

They're all pretty dismissive of anything to do with Health & Safety and there are times when it's like I'm the only grown-up trying to stop the children from hurting themselves. Jeremy has even called me an H & S official before when he was annoyed but I was the stuntman and stunt co-ordinator making sure it all worked and they got to film another day. Richard Hammond got it — he used to laugh when he saw me on set after a while. He'd go:

'Oh no, what am I going to have to do now? I know it's going to be dodgy, it's the only reason they bring you in!'

He was right. And I've been brought it to help Richard and the others do dodgy things for about ten years. We'd first met on a windy airfield about a decade earlier when I simply turned up to do a job for the BBC. I didn't know *Top Gear*, didn't know the people, I just rocked up. And there were James and Richard, also there early. I knew they were sort of famous and I didn't want to be seen as obsequious but we got chatting. I mentioned I'd been in *Where Eagles Dare* and been shot by Clint Eastwood and then they looked at me in a different way. From then on James in particular would introduce me as 'This is the bloke who got killed by Clint Eastwood in Where Eagles Dare!'. We got on great after that.

But that first day we had a stunt to do. Jeremy Clarkson turned up, someone I did recognise, but when I talked to him he simply told me to go and talk to The Hamster. I had no idea who that was (It was Richard Hammond). Eventually we got sorted out and I was told they wanted to roll a Suzuki Carry, a small, narrow van. They'd put weight up high in the roof so if turned sharply by Richard it should flop on its side. That wasn't the problem. The problem was that Richard had agreed to wear a crash helmet, which he thought was a sensible move.

That's about the worst thing to do with a simple roll onto its side, as the extra weight of the helmet was going to wrench his neck even more than the crash. I told him he was looking at serious whiplash. But he wouldn't take it off and he wouldn't wear a doughnut round his neck because of continuity with shots they already had. They did the shot. Richard got massive whiplash.

Maybe the fact that I'd warned him this would happen had some effect, because I ended up being called in to do other stunts until I was a regular in the background of the *Top Gear* series, year after year. Which meant I was involved in the utterly bizarre plan — even by their standards — to launch a Reliant Robin from a space rocket. It was 'reckoned' that because it was sort of pointed at the front it would fly, so they added stubby wings and a tail, and then this amazing bunch of rocketeers built the rocket.

They were actually an incredible bunch of blokes. I'd worked with them before on an earlier *Top Gear* episode where they sent a Mini off a ski jump in Lillehammer with rockets attached to the car. The way that Mini took off and landed was just perfect. We didn't have anyone in it but it flew and landed so smoothly you could actually have done the stunt with a driver.

So I rated these rocket men, and they spent months building this proper rocket that was going to launch the Robin (with wings attached) to about 1500ft. At that point bolts would explode and the car would then separate from the rocket and glide back to Earth, controlled by one of them via radio control. What could possibly go wrong?

The launch was from the Royal Artillery base at Otterburn in Northumberland. All day there were delays and problems, but it gave me to time to get everyone set. There were proper concrete bunkers there for observation, but there had to be a camera crew outside to film the rocket in the air, so my job was to ensure they stayed safe. Eventually the rocket went up, and it looked spectacular.

Unfortunately, at the top of the arc the Robin didn't separate from the rocket, which was now depleted. The whole thing started to come back down at a massive lick and I was trying to work out whether I needed to pull the guy off the camera, knowing that would completely wreck the shot. I kept looking up and looking at the crew, working out angles, and I decided we'd be just about okay. It landed about 100 yards away and just buried itself in the peat. You could see the back end of the Reliant, but the rest was completely buried in the ground. We got the shot.

Not all the stunts were quite so hairy, some were simply funny. Like the one where they converted a train with three carriages to run with first class, second class and scum class carriages. Scum class was just straw on the floor and a toilet bolted out the back on a platform in the open air.

The train was pulled by a Jaguar on rails, with Jeremy driving. At one point the idea was that the train would pull into a siding just as another train comes head on. It would miss the Jaguar but hit the carriages. I was up for driving the Jag but the railway bosses wouldn't let us do it. So instead they found something else for me to do.

They decided they wanted a shot of the train rattling along at 30mph with me sitting on the toilet (outside the rear of the last carriage) reading a paper with my trousers down. Horribly similar to the scene in *GoldenEye*. Great, I thought, I'm getting typecast, I'm 'the sitting on the bog guy'.

There was another Bond connection. In *The Man with the Golden Gun* the Bond team did the very first corkscrew leap in a car, something which became known as the Astro Spiral Jump. A car takes off and barrel-rolls through the air before landing on its wheels again. *Top Gear* decided it needed to reproduce this stunt. We didn't have a big budget or the access to computer modelling. Apparently the fact that the original Astro Spiral Jump was the very first computer-modelled stunt ever used in a Bond film was not really considered relevant.

We had some earth, a pipe ramp and an MG Maestro. We placed the pipe ramp on an earth ramp at what we thought was the right angle to launch it up and over. We then had to work out where to build a huge ramp where the Maestro would land. And work out what angle that ramp should be to catch the car as it rolled in to land. We used the backs of several envelopes and fag packets.

Then we got the cameras rolling, strapped stuntman Derek Lea into the Maestro and watched him head for the pipe ramp. We all crossed our fingers. Incredibly, it worked, we'd actually done the calculations right, and the Maestro flew beautifully through the air and landed in one piece. We were thrilled. The producers were horrified.

'Oh no,' they said, 'that's not what we wanted. We wanted a massive fail.'

So we had to go back to the drawing board, and alter the angles on the pipe ramp and the speeds and stuff and then, happily, it did fail spectacularly. The result made Derek's eyes revolve and water a bit, but that was just a typical piece of *Top Gear* silliness.

Like the Snowbine Harvester. We filmed that up in the snow and dark of Norway. It was a really sensible idea – a combine harvester with the blades removed and replaced by a snow plough and with a snow-clearing device at the rear. A flamethrower in fact. With Jeremy on the flamethrower, it was obviously only a matter of time before a lot more than snow got torched. At one point a man is walking down the road with his skis over his shoulder and the next moment he's on fire, trying to put out the flames on his ski suit. Guess who that was.

By the time *The Grand Tour* came around there was a lot more budget available, although a lot of the budget went on the two tents that they travelled with. It was about half a million quid or something silly just to transport them and put them up on location, because there was a convoy of trucks needed and about four days of set-up.

But the gags were still pretty silly. Which is fine, but on one stunt I nearly crossed the line and did something silly myself. We were in Dubai playing with a vehicle that was absolute catnip to the boys. The Ripsaw Extreme Vehicle 2 is a civilian version of a US military reconnaissance light tank. They've removed the weapons, upped the horsepower and produced a tracked vehicle you can buy which gets to 60mph in 3.5sec, on its way to a top end of 80mph.

The idea was that this thing would be perfect for a Dubai shopping mall. Particularly if it came smashing through a wall and charged around at high speed. We had the tank the other side of a 'solid' yellow wall, and we had extras dotted around, ready to run about in shock when the vehicle appeared. But it still seemed to lack something. So I decided that what I'd do was walk across in front of the wall, right by it, just before the Ripsaw came through.

This wasn't necessarily the most sensible thing to do since I couldn't see the tank although I could hear it – however, it needed only a very short run-up. They cued me in and I just walked across but I'd only just cleared the wall before it was smashed to bits by the tank rampaging through. It really was right behind me, and potentially that could have been very silly indeed. I really ought to know better.

Despite all the giggles, *Top Gear* and *Grand Tour* have always been a big pressure job, with everything moving at speed. When the three boys are all together there's a lot of piss-taking, which is fine, but it sometimes gets a bit over the top. Filming with them individually is a more relaxing affair, although when Jeremy gets nervous before an important bit of filming or a stunt he starts getting bad-tempered and that's when he shouts at people.

But recently I did a film just with Jeremy and then it was nicer and funnier again. We were in France where he was dressed as a caricature French traffic cop complete with moody moustache. As one of the producers, he'd written the gags along with fellow producer Andy

Wilman. Jeremy can be quite authoritarian in producer mode, but I've noticed something after working with him for a while.

We rehearse stuff, fine-tune it and get to the point of filming it – and then Jeremy will come in and he'll see another angle. He's done it numerous times, which is really inconvenient but I see exactly what he's talking about and the end result is simply funnier. He's very good at 'less is more'.

An example. So Jeremy is 'le speed cop' in the South of France and he's chasing these two blokes who've robbed the bank. They're wearing rubber masks to look like Hammond and May and they're driving a De Tomaso Pantera. There's the obligatory car chase through this village and at one point Jeremy comes screaming down a hill. At the bottom there is a café, with a load of French cyclists having a drink, with all their bicycles lined up outside. You can see where this is going.

We were set up for the gag of him swinging in broadside to wipe out all the bikes as he's driving away. Then Jeremy arrives and he watches his stunt double rehearsing the gag. And then he decides it would be funnier if he broadsided one way, knocking over a single bike, then puts it in reverse, deliberately drives over all the bikes and then goes 'Ooops' and then heads off.

That was a bit of a drag as we had to move everything around, including putting the bikes in a different position, and we hadn't rehearsed it that way. When we did, the stunt driver was too nervous of actually hitting the bikes and he'd stop before he'd actually touched them. Jeremy decided he needed to have a go, and the cameras were rolling.

He nailed it first time. He slipped the car round, just tipped the first bike, went back over the whole lot and drove away, all in one shot. It was absolutely spot on, you could not have done it any better, and it was all done in one take.

He's a clever man and I think he's also written and presented two of the best documentaries that I've ever seen: the one on the St Nazaire Raid and the one on the Victoria Cross won by his father-in-law at Arnhem. Not forgetting his one on the Arctic convoys either.

Richard Hammond has a really good sense of humour and it makes the whole thing easier when he's around. He's good company and keeps things relaxed. James May is as you see him. He has a lovely, quirky sense of humour and a very good brain. We've bonded over old motorcycles, although most of his collection is Japanese — we all have our cross to bear. He and I nearly got to make a documentary for the Bovington Tank Museum, as we both like tanks too, but sadly that hasn't happened yet.

But at least that allows me to stop talking about cars and talk about tanks.

21

SOUND AND FURY

'Best job I ever had.' Wardaddy, Fury

Best war film I never worked on? *Band of Brothers*. I really, really wanted to work on that series, but I was so busy filming on *Captain Correli's Mandolin* in Kefalonia that I couldn't get back to audition for the series. As you'll know if you've read this far, I've worked on lots of war films which included tanks, and even other films that included tanks, like *GoldenEye*. But there have been a couple that really do stand out. And not just because both featured a Tiger tank.

The first film, and the one with the worse Tiger, was *Saving Private Ryan*, a Spielberg film that I felt I had to work on as they'd gone to so much effort to make it look realistic and accurate. Luckily I got a gig on it and we went off to Ireland to shoot the D-Day scenes. Those were so like the real thing that in America the US Veterans Affairs department needed to set up a special number to deal with the increase in calls from traumatised vets, while other veterans left the cinemas early as it was just too like their memories.

I spent most of my time on the film in the village of Ramelle, where the final battle scenes were shot. Actually the village didn't exist in real life – all the others did – so Ramelle was built in the studio in Hertfordshire, complete with river. Some of it was later used when they were filming *Band of Brothers* – that's about as close as I got to the HBO mini-series.

I came on set thinking I knew what would be needed. I'd worked on Spielberg films before, like with *Indiana Jones*, and he used to operate on a very rigid shooting schedule which matches up with an animated storyboard that's been prepared earlier. But on *Saving Private Ryan* I saw four camera units, all in different places shooting different stuff. This was definitely going to be different.

The first scene I was involved in was the first time we meet Matt Damon as Private Ryan. He and others shoot up a German half-track, an Sd Kfz 251, and I was the driver. Actually it was a post-war Czech OT-810 but only uber-geeks like me would notice. I got an idea of the attention to detail when I was issued with a complete German uniform as the driver. I would be looking through a letterbox, nobody would be able to see me. It could have been a monkey in a wet suit for all that anyone would see, but I had a complete outfit to wear.

My instructions were to drive until the explosion went off, and then to continue to roll it on for another ten yards or so before grinding to a halt. The special effects man said 'You may need to block your ears a bit', which was all the warning I needed. I put in ear plugs with ear protectors, all under the helmet, but I couldn't do too much or I wouldn't hear the signal to go. I also made sure I was wearing gloves and was well covered. I was ready.

The explosion was loud, so loud it made my head shake. It was like being in a dustbin with six blokes smashing the outside with baseball bats. I held it together enough to do as instructed and came out of there with my German helmet vibrating like a gong.

Next scene was further along in the battle in Ramelle, where I was driving a German self-propelled gun. The scene was that the Americans up on the balcony throw down Molotov cocktails at the crew in the open fighting compartment above and behind me. They were real, bottles and fuel, the whole deal, and the men above were smeared with goop so they'd burn nicely. In theory I was tucked up all cosy in my driving compartment, with a shut hatch above me. Theories are great.

The reality was that I could see daylight round the hatch and I knew if a bottle missed above then I was going to have burning petrol coming in on me. Which was why I was wearing a full fire suit, while a small blanket of fireproof material was draped over my lap. A CO_2 extinguisher completed my preparations, which I hoped wouldn't be needed.

I was focusing on driving, since I needed to do the same thing, drive on a short distance after the bang, before coming to a stop. I heard the bangs of the Molotovs landing and it all kicked off. Inevitably, burning petrol started trickling in from the hatch right above my head.

Soon there was a little puddle of it burning merrily away on the blanket on my lap. I managed to keep driving while reaching for the

CO_2 extinguisher and set it off. Now my family jewels had gone from burning hot to freezing cold and I was still trying to look through the slit and to keep going. That was an interesting experience.

The next vehicle I drove was the Tiger tank, which as many know was actually based on a Russian T-34, and didn't really look totally authentic. Gary Powell, whom I'd taught to drive the T-55 on *GoldenEye*, did most of the Tiger driving, but I was needed for the shot where the track gets blown off by a 'sticky bomb'. That bit was fine. Less fine was the follow-up where Tom Hanks blasts his Tommy gun through the driver's vision slit.

It was actually quite a hard vehicle to control, and even changing gear was a trial, before someone fires a full burst of blanks in your face. Tom Hanks is a really kind bloke and he came up beforehand and was concerned about what it would be like for me when he fired a whole magazine. I told him it would be fine.

I wore all the ear protection I could muster, and as he approached I ground the tank into neutral and ducked down as much as I could. Even so it was a simply massive noise and blast in that confined space. Once again I came out ringing like a church bell. I can't understand why my hearing's not so good these days.

Bev (and Jordan, who was four at the time) came to watch the filming one day, and at one point I was carrying Jordan across the bridge on the set. There was a very rare and obscure German tracked motorcycle called a Kettenkrad parked across the bridge. As we approached it, Steven Spielberg was coming across the bridge in the opposite direction just as Jordan shouted out 'Look Daddy, a Kettenkrad!'

Spielberg stopped in his tracks and asked: 'How does she know that?' (Kettenkrad being quite an advanced word for a four-year-old.) I explained that I had one in my collection at home and she'd ridden in one many times. Jordan was also well known in our local Sainsbury's for singing World War I marching songs while being transported up and down the aisles in a backpack. A basic grounding in all things military from an early age!

⊙ ⊙ ⊙

That was back in 1998 so it's a bit of leap forward now to 2014, when *Fury* was released. I was tank crew supervisor on that film, which for much of the time meant looking after the five Shermans and their crews. Some of the tanks had been used in *Saving Private Ryan* so they were old friends, but the crews were all new. The director, David Ayer, wanted total authenticity, so the tank commanders were mostly ex- British Army tankies who'd seen military action in Afghanistan. They didn't want to be told how to command and crew the vehicles, but I had to get them to understand that the film world is a bit different to the real world. The drivers were mostly the owners of the vehicles and knew their mechanical quirks well enough to adjust things in time to make the scenes work.

The film made all the cast go on Boot Camp and that included the multi-millionaire actors like Brad Pitt and Shia LaBeouf. It was pretty tough, run by a US Special Forces adviser and a British ex-tank commander who had served in Bosnia and Afghanistan. Nobody got a free pass but I must say I was impressed at the way they all threw themselves into it.

All the actors were there from Page 1. Brad was there every day, a totally professional bloke. He wanted to learn about the guns and the tanks. He was totally into it. I talked to him many times and he's extraordinary. He never breaks eye contact. You know when you're having a conversation with him and that's refreshing.

Mind you, he and I got off to a potentially tricky start. On the first day on the film, I had my military Harley-Davidson there as set dressing. Brad immediately asked who it belonged to and could it be bought? I pointed out that it was mine and even he, Brad Pitt, didn't have enough money to buy that bike as I'd had it since 1970 and ridden all over many European battlefields on it.

He asked the same question the next day about buying it and, at the risk of being thrown off the film, I said jokingly: 'Which bit of "fuck off" didn't you understand yesterday?'. He laughed and eventually I found one for him, which he bought at the end of the film.

But like I say, all the actors were all in. When there was a scene with the tank that only needed Brad, Shia LaBeouf would come along even though it was a scene he wouldn't be seen in. He'd be in his tracksuit but he'd be there in the tank. The others would do the same, they functioned as a crew.

Shia actually stank. He didn't wash for the whole film I don't think, taking method acting to a new high, literally. He'd sit there smoking his fags. They all got grubby and covered in oil and stuff, it's not all make-up. These were 70-year-old machines, maintained well but a lot of the dirt and oil was just from moving around in these tanks.

They would all be like real crews and spend a lot of time in 'Fury'. They would eat in the tank, piss into ammo boxes inside the tank, they'd just get their food and disappear back inside, Brad included.

It was difficult because I had to get all the actors and then make them get in and out of the tank continuously for 20 minutes at a time so that they would learn exactly the best and quickest way to get in and out, where the handholds were and so on, so it looked convincing. Because that's what being a tank crew is all about: how quickly you can get into the tank to get away from small-arms fire and how quickly you can get out if the tank brews up.

Once filming started, my stress levels really went up because I was dealing with old, valuable machines where the drivers couldn't see much, and they were moving around lots of people, some of them Hollywood superstars. I organised the order of movement on set, sorting speed, continuity, that sort of thing. We worked for four months, mostly 10-12 hour days with lunch out of a box in the hand.

The thing that made the process work reasonably safely was a small electronic box hanging around my neck. If I hit the button then it shut down the engine in every tank and applied the brakes. Obviously I didn't want to do that often, but if a tank driver drove over a half dozen men he wouldn't even feel it. I only had to use the button twice. Once when the Shermans were rapidly retreating as the Tiger fired on them, and they were about to smash into a line of trees they couldn't see, so I shut them down. The second time, some of the infantry were walking alongside the tanks in a narrow alley and they just weren't concentrating, and I could see one Sherman just about to impact the guy and push him either into the wall or under the treads.

That Tiger of course was the star of the show. It wasn't some mocked-up vehicle, it was the only running Tiger in the world, the famous '131' captured in Tunisia. It normally living a pampered life at the Bovington Tank Museum. It looks great in the film, but in the metal it's really awe-inspiring, particularly when it's running its 23-litre Maybach V12 engine. The sound was something else.

However, we had to be very careful with it, as it's made of 70-year-old metal. We weren't allowed to turn it hard on the ground as it would put too much strain on the gearboxes. So we had to make a curved platform area filled with concrete and just loosely covered with earth so the tank could turn without strain. Since this was in a farmer's field, they had to then take all the concrete up again once we'd finished the 64 days of filming – that must have been a job.

It was all fairly hard work in mostly grim conditions, lots of rain and mud, but there were scenes there I'd have paid to watch. As far as I was concerned, I would never, in my lifetime, see four Shermans driving in a field, with a real Tiger firing its main armament, the explosions, the noise – it was the opportunity of a lifetime.

And we got the tank back to Bovington in one piece. Maybe even in better condition than when it arrived. If you want to see it now, that's where you'll have to go, to Dorset.

22

LOOKING FORWARD

'Always think with your stick forward.'
Aviation pioneer Amelia Earhart

I've long been a fan of The Tank Museum at Bovington, but that moved up to another level in about 2007 when I was taken down there by a mate who ran a charitable foundation. I got involved as it was thought I might be able to bring in some friends with showbiz connections to help raise the profile of this terrific museum. I ended up being a member of the fundraising committee, which at the time was trying to raise several million for a new wing to the museum.

At that stage I was doing *Top Gear* and I persuaded James May to go down and help make a short advertising video. That worked, and it raised the gate hugely, even though it was only shown locally.

I was then asked to do another video in their series of people choosing their five favourite tanks. This is a series you can find on YouTube, with people like YouTuber Lindybeige, comedian Al Murray – and yours truly. Last time I looked it had had over 300,000 views, which is just ridiculous but there you go. I still go down and do charity talks and so on to help them run the museum – well worth a visit.

In 2000, I was asked to present a new series for Sky called *Wheels at War*. We made the pilot out in Germany at the end of *Enemy at the Gates*. *Wheels at War* was to be an eight-part series covering different military vehicles from the main adversaries. The pilot was on the German BMW and Zundapp motorcycle combinations and the others were going to cover tanks, field cars, amphibians, half-tracks and so forth. Just before we were due to start the remaining episodes, Sky withdrew a huge amount from the budget, which meant we'd have all been working for nothing, so we walked away. The pilot episode is still being shown as I get emails from all over the world from friends saying they've just 'seen it again'.

In fact public speaking engagements are something I seem to be doing more of. Instead of setting myself on fire and falling off a building I get to talk about it instead. So far I've done everything from the Round Table to the London Guildhall, and even a talk to Coca-Cola in Warsaw. What I enjoy most about it is always the Q&A afterwards.

People have such a love for films but it's been an education for me realising how little the general public knows or understands about the industry. They just love to know about some of the iconic films I've had the privilege to work on, particularly the things that go on behind the scenes. They love to hear about some of the screen greats like Lee Marvin or Steve McQueen, but you have to choose your audience.

I did a talk recently at a literary society and there were some older people but also a few sons and daughters. When I realised that the youngsters hadn't even heard of actors like that, nor even of Harrison Ford or that era, then I changed the talk a bit to make sure they felt included.

I like to think that after nearly 50 years in the business I can talk to a diverse range of people and make sure it's not just all about me. I love interacting with people who have a little bit of knowledge, and you may be able to share something about their favourite film and open the door to tell them more about it.

I want to infuse the whole thing with humour, while keeping the stars alive. But I don't want it to become an 'I-Fest' as that's not what I'm all about, instead it's about giving people funny stories, or interesting stories or sometimes, dare I say it, thrilling stories. I think it's something I'll be doing more of and I can't wait.

Because, let's face it, I don't mind doing a few fire jobs a year or whatever, but I'm now quite happy to 'point the finger' and help others to do the stunts I've spent decades practicing. Also that leaves a bit more room for someone else to step up in what is now a crowded field. As the Chair of the British Stunt Register I'm concerned that there are more than 400 people on that Register and there simply isn't enough work for them all, even though there is more work than ever across all the new platforms. Governments have helped with more attractive tax breaks for filming in the UK too. Studios have literally never been busier in Britain, with new stages going up all the time. But there are still a lot of stuntmen and women who want the work.

We've also got robots, CGI and who knows what else to contend with. But people still like knowing a stunt was done for real. The more easily it can be replicated by a ten-year-old with the right software, the more the real deal has value. You only have to see the popularity of EPK films – Electronic Press Kits – which give you featurettes on how films were made, trailers and so on, to understand that. As CGI becomes more common I do think we're going back to reality, where a spectacular stunt, like some of the Bond gags, has real value now and in the future.

When you think of Rick Sylvester in *The Spy Who Loved Me*, after an incredible ski chase hurtling off the snowy cliff in his skis, only for his parachute to eventually open – now that's a gag that people still remember. If it was done with CGI it would have no emotion, no humanity.

And, while there are lots of animated and CGI characters, some of them are based on motion capture, where someone goes through the motions while wearing a suit with lots of data capture points on it – like Andy Serkis did to create Gollum in *Lord of the Rings*. So you may not appear in the film, but you're still being employed as a stunt performer.

I set one up last year, with what would be people swinging through the trees and smashing into things and stuff. For three days I had the stunt performers swinging from scaffolding that would be transformed into trees, with the performers wired up with hundreds of data-gathering points. They say that there's a quirkiness about the way that a human body moves that can't yet be replicated by electronics, there's a grittiness that is just real.

And those human bodies are the stunt performers who've featured in some of the greatest films of the last century. Yet they've never got official recognition. There are awards ceremonies for actors, supporting actors, camera work, you name it, but not for the stuntmen and women who've put their lives on the line. We've been left out in the cold, and we're a bit sore about that.

We do have the Taurus World Stunt Awards, which is a big deal once a year, a huge awards ceremony backed by Red Bull, but that's

22   *On the set of* Fury *with Brad Pitt on my BMW. He wanted to buy it. He couldn't.*

23   *Tank crew co-ordinator on* Fury *meant I was as busy as a one-armed paper hanger.*

24-5 *Blasting a Reliant Robin into the sky was clearly a stupid idea, but a lot of very clever people made it happen. My job was to keep them alive. Top Gear at its zaniest.*

26 *Home on the range with my Kettenkrad tracked motorcycle and the two faithful Ridgebacks, Emma and Elsa.*

27 *I was as fit as a butcher's dog back in the day. Although, to be fair, I can still fall into water pretty easily.*

28 *Driving the camera car, a Mitsubishi Evo VIII, on* Rush *with Director Ron Howard in the passenger seat. With 120kg of camera gear set up asymmetrically, with priceless race cars all around on a fast, wet track, it was really quite 'interesting'.* Photo credit: Andy Harriss, MSS.

29 *Dressed as a baddie – you can tell by the disturbing moustache – on* Indiana Jones and the Last Crusade *with stuntmen Malcolm Weaver and Billy Horrigan.*

30 *With Jackie Chan – this photo includes two fans.*

31 *Rehearsing a speedboat to helicopter transfer for* Bergerac *in Jersey.*

32 *My first 'fire job' for a medical burn salve product in 1974.*

33 *My motley crew of 'stunties' on* Captain Corelli's Mandolin.

34 *Discussing the next shot using the Saladin-based dummy T-55 in St Petersburg on* GoldenEye.

35 *Celebrating Jordan's first birthday with Bev in Russia on GoldenEye. Behind is the T-55, which has just collapsed a big monument onto itself.*

36-9 *Being fired off an air ram in the middle of an explosion for* Indiana Jones and the Last Crusade. *Credit: Nrinda Dudwar.*

40 *Getting blown up again. You flick the bars and the front of the weighted sidecar digs into a spike in its nose and hello sky, hello ground.* The Dirty Dozen Next Mission.

41 *Dodger, my faithful companion, who was with me on every film set. Usually by the food wagon.*

not recognised by the rest of the film industry. So we're trying to change all that.

We're trying to get events like the Baftas in the UK and the Motion Picture Academy in the US to recognise stunts as a separate award. We're hoping that within the next year or two both academies will recognise stunt performing as an awards category. We think it's time.

But for me personally it may sound terribly corny but it's been such a privilege to work with some really extraordinarily talented people. A few of them have been actors.

However, I've seen people who've done everything right, and it just hasn't worked one way or another. Luck has been such a stranger to them. I've been lucky, I really appreciate that, and if you're going to be a stunt performer that's one quality you're going to need – and it's the one we can't teach.

23

HOW TO BE A STUNT PERFORMER

'A lot of people ask me when I do a stunt: "Jackie, are you scared?"
Of course I'm scared. I'm not Superman.' Actor Jackie Chan

So you want to be a stunt performer? Maybe you're daydreaming about it after reading this book, maybe you're serious – either way, this is how you get to be a fully paid-up member of the British Stunt Register.

First off though, let's deal with another of those frequent questions I get: Isn't it a glamorous life? Certainly it can be, but the reality is often so, so different. Like, for example, when I was being all glamorous doubling for Harrison Ford on *Force 10 From Navarone*. I was doubling for a superstar, and we were on location in Montenegro – how glamorous is that?

The reality was that the small team of stuntmen weren't put in the same hotel as the grown-ups, we were miles away in a far more seedy establishment. It was in the winter so it was absolutely freezing – again. My room, which would be home for weeks, was about 10x6ft, with a cot bed, a three-legged table wedged in a corner and a chair. The chair was handy because you could use it to stand on to see out the window. There was a bit of pipework in the corner, roughly boxed in.

It hadn't taken long to explore the delights of my room, so I went down to reception just as a furious member of the team, the stills guy Laurie Ridley, stomped back into the lobby. He demanded the manager came with him to his room and naturally we all went along too. In his room, he peeled back the thin mattress and there was a dead rat that must have got caught between the springs and the mattress when someone jumped on the bed. It had clearly been dead for some time. Laurie demanded to know what the manager was going to do about it.

The manager peeled the dried rat off the springs, walked over to the balcony window that Laurie had, opened the window and threw the corpse down into the street. He made a gesture that clearly showed he thought the whole incident had been satisfactorily dealt with, and walked out. I went back to my room and put on all my clothes so I could get some sleep.

The next night when I got back to my room the pipe in the corner had burst. A small wooden inspection door in the covering boxwork had been blown open by the thin jet of icy cold water that was spraying across my room. Judging by the state of the plaster on the opposite wall, it had been hit by this jet for some time. It had soaked the area around the light switch as well as the threadbare carpet. I went to get the manager.

He came, he saw, he went away. He returned with a hammer and some nails. He nailed the inspection door shut although you could hear the water now hitting the back of it and pouring down to who knows where. He made a gesture that clearly showed he thought the whole incident had been satisfactorily dealt with, and walked out. I finally managed to get a plumber to sort it out after a couple of days of listening to freezing water torture and trying not to use the light switch. See what I mean – glamour, glamour, glamour.

Right, now we've dealt with that, let's look at how you can join this glamorous profession.

The standards are high – the British Action Academy reckons to join the British Stunt Register 'requires the dedication of a professional athlete'. New guidelines are being drawn up, but basically you need to have spent about 64 days in front of the camera as an extra or a walk-on part, to show that you understand the basics, like how to take a cue, which is stage left and right, which is upstage or downstage, and so on. You can get these parts through one of the many extras agencies, and they'll give you the contracts you'll need to show.

In some ways that's the easier part. The other part is showing you have the physicality for the role. That means, out of a list of about 21 sports, you need to be qualified in at least six. Badminton isn't one of them. You'll need to be proficient, to a high level, in things like motorcycling, skiing, parachuting, hang-gliding, diving and so on.

One of the six needs to be a fighting sport, like boxing, wrestling, martial arts or similar. Again, this needs to be well above the minimum standard if you're to be accepted in the Register.

You'll need to go on at least one of the three Health & Safety courses, and maybe a First Aid course as well. And you'll need your own personal insurance – actually that's not too bad as statistically stunt performers are a better risk outside work than the average man in the street.

If you've achieved all that then you come and meet us and, if you pass, you're in at the bottom rung of the Register. There are now five categories for you to progress through: probationary, stunt performer, senior stunt performer, assistant co-ordinator and, finally, co-ordinator.

If that sounds daunting – it is. It can easily take five or six years if you're starting from scratch and cost maybe £30,000 just to get in at the bottom. You need to demonstrate dedication to make it.

All of that is what you are, but who you are is even more important. After nearly 50 years in the business I've seen a lot of changes in the stunt industry. Back in the day there were a lot of Brits who'd been jackaroos in Australia, or rodeo riders in America, people who'd done jousting or boxing or who'd been in the military – particularly the Parachute Regiment.

Now you need a lot more dedication, because you have to do so much more to get on the Register. You'll have already read about how fitness has reached new peaks, but mental attitude is paramount. You have to feel you have the mental aptitude to control your own body. They say a good stuntman is ten feet in front of his body, and that's right.

A common stunt will be you hurtling through the air having been launched by an air ram. Maybe someone is out of position and you realise you're going to hit them. The cameras are rolling. So you could just shout, mess up the shot and then apologise. Or you twist in the air and windmill around so you just miss them. And maybe get an even better shot.

You need to be a team player and you need to pay permanent attention to detail. Assumption is the mother of all foul-ups. You have to check everything repeatedly before the stunt. If it's a car stunt, have you checked the car, have you checked the seatbelts, have you checked the airbags are turned off even if you've been told they are?

I do a lot of invigilation for young performers, and they write to me asking if I can do an observation and they usually write on a laptop or whatever. And sometimes their grammar is crap or they can't put the full stop in the right place. They haven't double-checked their work and that matters.

I'm fussy about these things because, if you're a hundred foot up it's the small details that will let you down. It's the difference between the stunt going well and you walking away happy, or you limping away or you being carried away in a meat wagon.

I look for people who are on time, and who aren't afraid to ask questions even if it might make them look silly. It's possible I'll have missed something, and if they speak up I value that.

I often get asked if you need to be brave to be a stuntman, but I think that's not the right word. It's about confidence and calculation, because the very word 'brave' conjures up a response to something which is not necessarily thought through.

Yes of course you need a degree of bottle, but confidence helps to control fear. Knowledge Dispels Fear – that's the motto of the Number 1 Parachute Training School. If you have an idea of what you are doing and what is possible it then becomes an exercise in calculated skill and risk rather than bravery. You weigh up the risks and the most important thing is knowing when to say 'No', because it's outside my capacity so, if I did it, it would be bravado and I would probably hurt myself.

There are some people out there who have come on to the Stunt Register and they've been around for a bit but, for one reason or another, after a couple of years they've discovered the work isn't out there for them. There can be many reasons for that. Some people just don't fit in, that's some indefinable thing which means perhaps they are not a team player or their skills are not quite advanced enough and when it's come to the testing time they have not been able to step up to the plate. People do lose their nerve occasionally.

The idea is to reduce the risks as much as possible but at the same time, by definition, a stunt is a stunt and if it was all safe, we wouldn't be the boys and girls we are now. But managing and bypassing as many as possible of the pitfalls is where the skill comes in.

Another question I often get asked is if I get scared. I wouldn't use that word, but I certainly get nervous before a big job, sometimes a couple of days before. Things like fire jobs don't really make my heart rate go up much as I've done so many and I have such confidence in my kit and the people around me. This really is a team effort.

But where some of it is outside your control, that's when it gets nerve-wracking. Like a knock-down. I'm not going to do any more of those, but that's where you get hit by a car. The car approaches at about 18mph and you know you have to get up on that bonnet, but as you hit the windscreen you might hit it at the wrong point or put an elbow through it, and then maybe you'll get kicked off the side or the back. You won't come out of a car hit without bruising, and there are lots of variables outside your control. When you've got a job like that coming up it definitely niggles away for a day and night or two. You know you're going to get a bang and bruises.

Bruises fade, but I'm old-fashioned enough that I don't really like seeing female stunt performers do that sort of job, largely because of the bruising. I struggle when watching a girl fall down a flight of stairs. Men can usually put pads on under their clothes, but for stunt women they're usually in a dress so they can't wear pads and they get bad bruising. If they're going out in a snappy little dress a couple of days later, they'll be bruised all over, which is perhaps more of an issue for them than for a bloke who's been similarly knocked about.

Back in the old days men used to double for women but now that is mostly forbidden. Although the Health & Safety Executive have said that safety is paramount, so if the stunt requires a specific skill, and nobody else has it, then a man can still double for a woman. They can even black-up for that matter, which we thought was completely out of bounds now. But the H & S Executive has put safety first, which is an interesting edict.

Women have to go through all the same hoops as the men, the same physical and mental requirements. And that is one big change over the last 20 years, how many stuntwomen have joined the Register. We have some phenomenal female performers, trapeze artists, hang glider pilots, motorbike riders, the lot. Although sadly one of our own, Olivia Jackson, recently lost her arm in a motorbike crash on *Resident Evil* when it all went wrong.

Overall, the whole playing field has been really levelled in terms of men and women performers and there are more and more women coming onto the Stunt Register. That means stuntmen won't have to do some of the stunts I had to do in the past, like the time I had to double an enormous female opera singer. I had the huge chiffon dress, the falsies, the blonde wig and a glittering tiara that was about two-feet wide at the top. I was sat in a tiny Fiat, with my head – and wig and tiara – sticking out through the sunroof. I had to drive down a flight of stairs while singing opera. Ah, what the new generation of stuntmen are going to miss.

But actually age itself isn't necessarily a barrier to a life doing stunts. You can still perform stunts in your 60s, 70s or 80s. A mate of mine is temporarily off work because he's getting a dodgy knee fixed. He's 73. About a month before writing this I was in Prague, for an American TV show called *Whiskey Cavalier*. I had to get a shotgun blast to the chest and then hit a table on the way down.

Except on the first take six of the nine detonators didn't go off, so we went for a second take. This time one of the detonators was up too high, too close to my face. When it went off it sliced upwards. After the explosion I could feel blood running down my face and into my collar, but it turned out they needed a third take. They'd flown me out there, they were depending on me, so you just have to suck it up and get on with it. I had a bruised face and couldn't shave for a week.

I must admit I did get back on my feet after the third take and think 'You're 70 you silly f***** what are you doing?'

And of course the answer to that is that action costs money. How much you get paid varies wildly but you can make a good living if all goes well. At the basic level you'll get a day rate for, say, being in a bar scene where there's a fight. You're part of the crowd at the bar, you throw some punches, you get hit, you fall over, all in a day's work. But if you're the guy who gets thrown over the bar or through the window then you'd get an adjustment to your daily fee, with the increase depending on how difficult or dangerous the stunt was.

You can make a decent income but sometimes the big set pieces get a really big adjustment. Something huge, like Wayne Michaels jumping off the dam in *GoldenEye* could be worth maybe $20,000 extra on top of the day rate. Frankly, for that stunt, it wasn't enough, but you get the idea. Commercials can – and certainly used to be – more steadily lucrative.

These days you tend to do the stunt and then you get a buy-out, so the company buys the rights to use that advert as it wishes for a period of time, like a year. That could be worth £10,000 or even £20,000 to you, which isn't bad for something that could all be done in a day. In the old days there was a system of residuals so every time the ad was shown you got a fee, based on all kinds of things like networks, country or whatever. I remember seeing myself in one commercial night after night, just waiting for a big fat cheque to come and dent the doormat. I did one job where the first repeat cheque in the 1980s was for £32,000.

But they don't pay you for nothing. As you might have read earlier, it can be a dangerous game even when things go right. And they don't always go right.

24

WHEN STUNTS GO WRONG

'Our bodies are apt to be our autobiographies.' Frank Gelett Burgess

It's incredible the number of ways things can go wrong – some of them mentioned in Chapter 8. Sometimes it's not even in a bad way, things just don't work out. Like you're in the middle of filming and an old boy appears in his pyjamas to complain. And he's holding a shotgun.

We were filming *Hanover Street*, which was one of my favourite films to work on. We were in the market town of Woodstock in Oxfordshire, where the town hall had been converted into a German headquarters, complete with enormous swastika flags. It's a lovely middle-class area, and we were driving round the streets at night, firing machine guns, power sliding motorbikes and sidecars and having a lovely time.

Then, late in the evening, this chap came out of his house near the town hall. We were all standing there with motorbikes and guns and German uniforms, and he walked up to us. We noticed he was wearing a paisley dressing gown and carrying a double-barrelled shotgun under his arm.

He demanded to know who was in charge. Being all tough and macho in our German uniforms, we shuffled our feet and pointed at the first assistant, who was actually a really nice guy. The old boy nodded and said:

'We had a notice sent round that there would be a certain amount of shooting and things going on but you would be finishing at 9.30pm. It is now 10.20pm and you are still shooting. Which could be my intention if it doesn't stop right now.'

The first assistant nodded. 'That's a wrap' he announced to us, and we all slunk off. It was so beautifully English, people are so nice in Woodstock.

You may have noticed in this book that some of the people I've grown wary of over the years are the special effects guys. That incident testing the exploding bridge bolts in *Hanover Street* was just a perfect example of why I've learned to watch and listen for the little clues when they're setting up an explosion for a gag. A classic example was on a film called *Underworld* with Denholm Elliott.

We were filming at St Catherine's Dock in London, before it was all converted, and we had the run of some of the old piers. This included an old Customs & Excise hut on one of the jetties. The scene was, our man runs up to the doorway of the hut, fires his machine gun through the open door and then lobs in a grenade. Gunfire, then an explosion.

Except I was watching the special effects man prep the steel pot that would contain the explosive and some debris as well as a bit of petrol, to simulate the grenade going off inside. I looked at the amount of petrol he was putting in and went and looked at the building again. As stunt co-ordinator, I saw it was a solid brick building with heavy steel mesh panels over the windows. It should do.

But I told the stuntman that when it came time for the 'grenade' to go off he had to be standing outside, with his back to the brickwork between the door and the window. And he should wear earplugs. To make things worse, there was a half-hour delay to filming so I knew the hut would be filling with ever more volatile petrol fumes. The special effects guy seemed perfectly happy with it all.

Well, they filmed the scene, and when the pot went off it blew the windows then the steel mesh covers completely out. It actually blew off the top of the thick steel pot – that's 9mm cast steel – out and away. The stuntman was okay as he'd been standing on the mark I'd set for him, but he looked a bit pale. The next day we were looking around the next dock over, some distance from where we'd been filming. And there was the jagged top of the steel pot - it had been blown at least 100 yards. Good thing the stuntman hadn't been standing in the doorway.

From London to Moscow. There were five of us, working on a stunt sequence for *The Bourne Supremacy*. Naturally, it was freezing cold, with snow just starting to melt to grey, dirty slush. And we were working with a second unit director known in the trade as Dangerous Dan.

Dan Bradley always wanted to get the shot, no matter what. But he wasn't the problem. The problem was that the cars we were meant to be driving were rubbish, sourced from a local company. Things got so bad that eventually we brought in a British vehicle co-ordinator, but before he turned up we were filming with cars that just didn't work properly. Jason Bourne – Matt Damon – had about half a dozen examples of the taxi he's meant to be driving, but only two of them had decent engines. When you're trying to get split-second gags going that's not helpful.

I was driving a police car, and it was such a dog that putting the brakes on would either slow the car or turn you through 90 degrees. Trying to get it right in snow and slush made things more exciting than we really wanted. Which would have been bearable if we'd been on a secure set.

The roads were meant to have been blocked off, with Russians standing on all the junctions to ensure the roads we were filming on stayed free of not just traffic but also pedestrians or anything else. It worked for about 20 minutes, then people's attention would start to wander and then pedestrians and cars would start appearing in shot in the background.

At one point I came round a corner in the police car, with the blue lights going and everything, going as quickly as I could. But instead of an empty bit of road there was a woman nonchalantly pushing a pram across the road in front of me. I thought if I slammed the brakes on there was a good chance the car would spin and collect both her and her baby, so I had to accelerate to try to get between her and the kerb ahead of her. I missed her and the pram and breathed a sigh of relief. When I looked in the mirror I saw her shouting and shaking her fist at me.

From the grubby snow of Russia to the exotic palm-tree desert of North Africa. Except it's not the Sahara, it's a wet beach in Essex in March. And the palm tree is plastic.

It was early in my stunt career and all I knew when I turned up was that I was going to get shot and fall out the back of a Jeep. It seemed straightforward enough, but I watched the special effects guy with some interest. He'd been in the game a long time, then left it to run a pub, and now he was back again. He was preparing the bullet effect to go on my torso.

You take a small aluminium or steel plate and tape a detonator to the plate. Then you tape on what looks like a condom filled with blood. Then you tape all that onto the stuntman, in this case me. The final element is to weaken the cloth over the detonator so when I got 'shot' the blast rips through the cloth and looks like a bloody hit.

The issue was that it was foggy and raining and cold – typical Sahara weather really. I couldn't believe that the tape would hold things in place but I was assured it would all be fine – again, being pretty new to all this, I simply shrugged and believed it.

I was on the back of the Jeep, firing away, with a wire up my leg to the detonator just under my rib cage. The detonator went off, I fell off the back of the Jeep and the director said 'Cut', and I lay thinking that it hurt more than it ought to. Sure enough, the detonator had worked round to the inside of the plate as the tape had got wet. It had detonated between the plate and my ribcage. I had a hole in my side that was suppurating plasma and blood.

I didn't feel great. But I felt a lot worse when I discovered we were making a softcore porn film, and now myself and another guy were meant to be having a bit of a session with a girl wearing a very skimpy nurse's outfit. I just laughed, feeling like I'd been run over by a horse.

That is a sensation I know all about. It was a Weetabix cereal commercial. I was doubling a vet, having a very bad day. He goes into a field to attend to hundreds of sheep and gets 'butted' over the hedge by a bull. That didn't go well, as I was fired over the hedge by an air ram and I landed badly, hurting my ankle. That was pretty much the high point of the day.

Various other disasters strike the vet as the commercial grinds on, and then we reached the last shot. I had to chase after a big horse, with a huge syringe in my hand. The idea was that I'm holding on to a long set of reins running behind the horse. The horse bolts and I get dragged across the field behind it. We had a particular horse booked for the shoot but he didn't turn up – maybe he was double-booked or had fallen out with his agent or something.

The horse that did turn up looked like a slow old carthorse and we were worried it wouldn't get into a gallop, so I asked the person looking after it what the horse really hated. Surprisingly, the answer was 'the sound of an aerosol can'! We instantly went off and found a big can.

It was February – have you noticed how often filming takes place in the cold? The ground was rock hard so I rigged the reins with 4mm steel cable, running them out of sight, so they could connect up to the harness I wore. This had a three-ring release so all I had to do was pull the release and the horse could bugger off into the next county without me once we'd got the shot.

I was still bothered about how hard the ground was, so I made sure I wore elbow, hip and knee pads and also a 'box' to protect my privates, since I knew I was going to get dragged. Time for Action. Off-camera there was the sound of an aerosol can. The idea was I'd run behind the horse for a few paces before falling over. No chance. That horse went from standstill to flat out in about two paces.

After the first pace I was horizontal in the air. The second pace I was on the frozen earth being dragged at speed. The friction against the hard ground was terrible, but for some reason it was particularly bad in the 'box'. My family jewels started to heat up uncomfortably.

The director kept holding the shot for a long time and I was really starting to cook in places I didn't want to cook. But then I heard the director shout 'Cut' and I went to release the harness. At that moment one of the horse's rear hooves flicked up a huge frozen cowpat into my face. It hit me like a soup plate, bang, and then it exploded. It turned out it was hard on the outside but soft in the middle. Like a good meringue.

I was stunned by the impact and completely blinded by cowshit, but I had released the traces and ground to a halt. I finally stood up, grabbing at my trousers. I wrenched them down, then my underwear, and threw the 'box' away. With one hand I was trying to get this muck out of my eyes and with the other I was fanning the family jewels, which were burning hot.

I could vaguely hear the director actually crying with laughter. It wasn't my finest moment. I stood there feeling pretty terrible and I thought: I'm 50 years old, I really shouldn't be doing this.

It was getting dark, and I was late for a dinner party at friends so I didn't have time to change. I was absolutely knackered when I got there, but made some jokes about my day. The first course was soup. As I looked down at it a chunk of cowpat I hadn't noticed fell out of my hair and into the soup. My how we laughed.

I'd fallen asleep at the table before the next course and they just left me sleeping and talked round me.

Oh yes, it's been a glamorous life so far.

PS My wife has a phobia about lobsters, snakes and being photographed.

Jordan wants to own a Jagdpanther.

'That's All I Have to Say About That.'
Forrest Gump

My Cv

('I see, Mr Dowdall. But – haven't you ever had a proper job?')

1 O Level (English Language)
Duke of Edinburgh Award Silver (Army Cadets)
Bertram Mills Circus (roustabout and occasional acrobat)
Kennings Car Hire (car washer)
Pride & Clarke Motorcycles (stripping bikes for used parts)
Harrods (packing toys over Christmas)
Bapty and Co (film armourer)
Minicab driver
Paratrooper (Champion Recruit)
Film extra with Ugly Agency and Havoc Stunt Agency
      (*Dr Who*, *Dixon of Dock Green*, *Colditz* etc)
2nd Assistant Director on commercials
Stuntman (from 1973 onwards)
Stunt co-ordinator and performer (from 1978 onwards)
Delivering cars across the USA
Occasional actor with dialogue
Camel Trophy film crew 1994 Guyana and Brazil
High-speed pursuit camera tracking vehicle driver (*Rush* etc)
After dinner speaker and historical consultant

Advertising Craft Awards 2001 – Best Stunt
Member of BAFTA
Member of the Academy of Motion Picture Arts
Hon Fellow of the BKSTS
Chair of The British Stunt Register

FILMOGRAPHY

2018
The Time Tree (Short) (stunt coordinator)
The Grand Tour (TV Series) (stunts – 2 episodes)
- It's a gas, gas, gas (stunts)
- Jaaaaaaaags (stunts)

2017
The Child in Time (TV Movie) (stunt coordinator)
The Gun Man (Short) (stunt coordinator)
Mindhorn (stunt performer)
Dark Signal (stunt driver)
London Has Fallen (assistant stunt coordinator: UK)

2015
Burnt (stunt performer)
Holby City (TV Series) (stunt coordinator – 4 episodes)
- An Eye for an Eye (2015) (stunt coordinator)
- Recovery Position (2013) (stunt coordinator)
- Ask Me No Questions (2013) (stunt coordinator)
- Spence›s Choice: Part Two (2013) (stunt coordinator)
Midsomer Murders (TV Series) (stunt coordinator – 1 episode)
- The Dagger Club (stunt coordinator)
Silent Witness (TV Series) (stunt coordinator – 2 episodes)
- Protection: Part 2 (stunt coordinator)
- Protection: Part 1 (stunt coordinator)

2014
Trollied (TV Series) (stunt coordinator – 2 episodes)

- Episode #4.8 (stunt coordinator)
- Episode #4.5 (stunt coordinator)

Shetland (TV Series) (stunts – 1 episode)
- Raven Black: Part 2 (stunts)

Jack Ryan: Shadow Recruit (stunts)

The Bletchley Circle (TV Series) (stunt coordinator – 1 episode)
- Blood on Their Hands: Part 1 (stunt coordinator)

Rush (pursuit precision driver)

2013

RED 2 (stunt performer)

Fast & Furious 6 (stunts – uncredited)

Welcome to the Punch (stunt performer)

2012

Tezz (stunt coordinator)

EastEnders (TV Series) (stunt coordinator – 2 episodes)
- Episode dated 10 April 2012 (stunt coordinator)
- Episode dated 30 March 2006 (stunt coordinator)

The Shoes: Time to Dance (Video short) (stunt coordinator)

Call the Midwife (TV Series) (stunt coordinator – 1 episode)
- Episode #1.6 (stunt coordinator)

Safe House (precision driver)

Milton Jones's House of Rooms (TV Series) (stunt coordinator – 1 episode)
- Paul (stunt coordinator)

2011

Johnny English Reborn (stunt performer)

One Day (stunt coordinator)

Harry Potter and the Deathly Hallows: Part 2 (stunts)

Blitz (stunt coordinator: additional shoot unit)

2010

The Little House (TV Series) (stunt coordinator – 2 episodes)
- Episode #1.2 (stunt coordinator)
- Episode #1.1 (stunt coordinator)

Harry Potter and the Deathly Hallows: Part 1 (stunts)

The Confession (Short) (stunt coordinator)

Wild Target (stunt coordinator)

Richard Hammond's Invisible Worlds (TV Mini-Series documentary)
   (stunt coordinator - 1 episode)
   - Off the Scale (stunt coordinator - uncredited)

M.I.High (TV Series) (stunt coordinator - 1 episode)
   - Don't Cook *Now* (stunt coordinator)

Rock & Chips (TV Series) (stunt coordinator - 1 episode)
   - Pilot (stunt coordinator)

2009

The Bill (TV Series) (stunt coordinator - 41 episodes, 2002 - 2009)
   (fight arranger - 1 episode, 2004) (stunt arranger - 1 episode,
   1989)

The Descent: Part 2 (stunt coordinator)

The Street (TV Series) (stunt performer - 1 episode)
   - Scar (stunt performer)

Blackwater (Short) (stunt coordinator)

2008

The Royal (TV Series) (stunt coordinator - 1 episode)
   - Home from the Hill (stunt coordinator)

Tenner (Short) (stunts)

Top Gear (TV Series) (stuntman - 2 episodes, 2008) (stunt
   coordinator - 1 episode, 2008)
   - Episode #12.1 (stunt coordinator)
   - Episode #11.2 (stuntman)
   - Police Car Challenge (stuntman)

Dead Set (TV Mini-Series) (stunt coordinator - 1 episode)
   - Episode #1.5 (stunt coordinator)

RocknRolla (stunt coordinator)

City of Vice (TV Mini-Series) (stunt coordinator - 5 episodes)
   - Episode #1.5 (stunt coordinator)
   - Episode #1.4 (stunt coordinator)
   - Episode #1.3 (stunt coordinator)
   - Episode #1.2 (stunt coordinator)
   - Episode #1.1 (stunt coordinator)

2007
National Treasure: Book of Secrets (stunts: London unit)
Death Defying Acts (stunt coordinator)
The Deaths of Ian Stone (stunt coordinator)
And When Did You Last See Your Father? (stunt coordinator)
Dalziel and Pascoe (TV Series) (stunt coordinator – 5 episodes)
   – Under Dark Stars: Part 2 (2007) (stunt coordinator)
   – Under Dark Stars: Part 1 (2007) (stunt coordinator)
   – The Cave Woman: Part 2 (2006) (stunt coordinator)
   – The Cave Woman: Part 1 (2006) (stunt coordinator)
   – A Death in the Family: Part 1 (2006) (stunt coordinator)
Straightheads (stunt coordinator)
Hotel Babylon (TV Series) (stunt coordinator – 1 episode)
   – Episode #2.8 (2007) ... (stunt coordinator)
Flood (stunt coordinator: UK)
Shameless (TV Series) (stunt coordinator – 1 episode)
   – Episode #4.8 (stunt coordinator)
The Good Night (stunt coordinator)

2006
The Amazing Mrs Pritchard (TV Series) (stunt coordinator – 1 episode)
   – Episode #1.1 (stunt coordinator)
Stormbreaker (stunts)
Green Wing (TV Series) (stunt coordinator – 2 episodes)
   – Episode #2.8 (2006) (stunt coordinator)
   – Christmas Special (2006) (stunt coordinator)

2005
The Golden Hour (TV Mini-Series) (stunt arranger – 2 episodes)
   – Episode #1.3 (stunt arranger)
   – Episode #1.1 (stunt arranger)
Casualty @ Holby City (TV Series) (stunt arranger – 1 episode)
   – Interactive: Something We Can Do (stunt arranger)
Charlie and the Chocolate Factory (stunt coordinator – as James Dowdall)
The Hitchhiker's Guide to the Galaxy (stunt coordinator)
Sahara (stunt player)
The Descent (stunt coordinator)

2004
Frances Tuesday (TV Movie) (stunt coordinator)
Wimbledon (stunt coordinator)
Enduring Love (stunt coordinator: second unit)
Finding Neverland (stunt performer)
The Bourne Supremacy (stunt driver)
Agent Cody Banks 2: Destination London (stunt coordinator)
Sex Lives of the Potato Men (stunt driver)
If Only (stunt driver)

2003
Two Thousand Acres of Sky (TV Series) (stunt coordinator – 1 episode)
    – Episode #3.5 (stunt coordinator)
Faking It (TV Series) (stunt director – 1 episode)
    – Faking it... as a Stuntman (stunt director)
Suspicion (TV Movie) (stunt coordinator)
My Hero (TV Series) (stunt coordinator – 1 episode)
    – Space Virus (stunt coordinator)
Murder in Mind (TV Series) (stunt coordinator – 4 episodes)
    – Justice (2003) (stunt coordinator)
    – Regrets (2002) (stunt coordinator)
    – Flashback (2002) (stunt coordinator)
    – Passion (2002) (stunt coordinator)
I'll Be There (stunt coordinator) / (stunt performer)
Cambridge Spies (TV Mini-Series) (stunt arranger – 4 episodes)
    – Episode #1.4 (stunt arranger)
    – Episode #1.3 (stunt arranger)
    – Episode #1.2 (stunt arranger)
    – Episode #1.1 (stunt arranger)
Bright Young Things (stunts)
I'll Sleep When I'm Dead (stunt coordinator)
Red Cap (TV Series) (stunt coordinator – 2 episodes)
    – Crush (stunt coordinator)
    – H-Hour (stunt coordinator)
Capture the Castle (stunt coordinator)

2002
The Gathering (stunts)
Where Were We ... (Short) (stunt coordinator)
Clarkson: No Limits (Video documentary) (stunt driver)
Die Another Day (stunt performer)
The Heart of Me (stunt coordinator)
The Pianist (stunt coordinator)
Sweet Sixteen (stunt coordinator)
The Gathering Storm (TV Movie) (stunt coordinator)
Clocking Off (TV Series) (stunt coordinator – 1 episode)
  – Mark›s Story (stunt coordinator)

2001
The 51st State (stunt coordinator)
Messiah (TV Mini-Series) (stunts – 1 episode)
  – The Reckoning (stunts)
Captain Corelli's Mandolin (stunt coordinator)
Enemy at the Gates (stunt coordinator)

2000
Five Seconds to Spare (stunt coordinator)
Pandaemonium (stunt coordinator)
Quills (stunt coordinator)
Gangster No. 1 (stunt coordinator)
The Blind Date (stunt coordinator)

1999
The Escort (stunt coordinator)
The World Is Not Enough (stunts – uncredited)
Entrapment (stunt coordinator)
The War Zone (stunt coordinator)

1998
Cash in Hand (stunt arranger)
The Dance of Shiva (Short) (stunt arranger)
Supply & Demand (TV Mini-Series) (stunt coordinator – 5 episodes)
  – Blood Ties: Part 2 (stunt coordinator)

- Blood Ties: Part 1 (stunt coordinator)
- Golden Goose: Part 2 (stunt coordinator)
- Golden Goose: Part 1 (stunt coordinator)
- Raw Recruit: Part 1 (stunt coordinator)

Little Voice (stunt double)

The Theory of Flight (stunt coordinator)

Saving Private Ryan (stunts)

Little White Lies (TV Movie) (stunt coordinator)

Casualty (TV Series) (stunt arranger - 4 episodes)
- Everlasting Love: Part 2 (1998) (stunt arranger)
- We Can Be Heroes (1998) (stunt arranger)
- Facing Up (1997) (stunt arranger)
- Bad Company (1997) (stunt arranger)

The Vicar of Dibley (TV Series) (stunt coordinator - 1 episode, 1998) (stunt co-ordinator - 1 episode, 1997)
- Love and Marriage (1998) (stunt coordinator)
- Engagement (1997) (stunt co-ordinator)

1997

The Woman in White (TV Movie) (stunts)

Tomorrow Never Dies (stunts)

The Borrowers (stunt coordinator)

Fairy Tale: A True Story (stunt coordinator)

Our Boy (TV Movie) (stunts)

Supply & Demand (TV Movie) (stunt coordinator)

1996

Daylight (stunts)

The English Patient (stunt supervisor)

Mary Reilly (stunt coordinator)

Different for Girls (stunt arranger)

1995

Restoration (stunts)

GoldenEye (stunts)

Hackers (stunt coordinator)

Richard III (stunt coordinator)

Prime Suspect: Inner Circles (TV Movie) (stunt coordinator)
Harry (TV Series) (stunt arranger - 1 episode)
   - Episode #2.1 (stunt arranger)
The Last Englishman (TV Movie) (stunts)

1994
Seaforth (TV Mini-Series) (stunt coordinator - 1 episode)
   - Under the Counter (stunt coordinator)
Between the Lines (TV Series) (stunt performer - 1 episode)
   - A Face in the Crowd (stunt performer)
Bloody Weekend (stunt coordinator)
Shopping (stunt coordinator)
Pie in the Sky (TV Series) (stunts - 1 episode)
   - A Matter of Taste (stunts)

1993
In the Name of the Father (stunts)
Screen One (TV Series) (stunts - 1 episode)
   - Wide-Eyed and Legless (stunts)
Splitting Heirs (stunts)

1992
Kinsey (TV Series) (stunt performer - 1 episode)
   - Conflicts of Interest (stunt performer)
Boon (TV Series) (stunt arranger - 1 episode)
   - Blackballed (stunt arranger)
Civvies (TV Series) (stunt performer - 3 episodes)
   - Episode #1.5 (stunt performer)
   - Episode #1.4 (stunt performer)
   - Episode #1.2 (stunt performer)

1991
Minder (TV Series) (stunt coordinator - 2 episodes)
   - The Coach That Came in from the Cold (stunt coordinator)
   - The Loneliness of the Long Distance Entrepreneur (stunt
   coordinator)
Smack and Thistle (TV Movie) (stunt coordinator)

Born to Ride (stunt coordinator) / (stunts)
Sleepers (TV Mini-Series) (stunt performer – 1 episode)
  – On the Run (stunt performer)
Agatha Christie's Poirot (TV Series) (stunts – 1 episode)
  – The Theft of the Royal Ruby (stunts)

1990
Medics (TV Series) (stunt arranger – 1 episode)
  – Alex (stunt arranger)
Bullseye! (stunts)
Nightbreed (stunts)
Bergerac (TV Series) (stunts – 1 episode, 1989) (stuntman – 1 episode, 1981)
  – Second Time Around (1989) (stunts)
  – Sea Changes (1989) (stunt arranger)
  – Picking It Up (1981) (stunt arranger / stuntman)

1989
Wilt (stunts)
Batman (stunts)
Indiana Jones and the Last Crusade (stunts)
The Tall Guy (stunt coordinator)

1988
Game, Set, and Match (TV Series) (stuntman – 1 episode)
  – London Match: Part 3 (stuntman)
The Dressmaker (stunt coordinator)
Hawks (stunts)
Rockliffe's Babies (TV Series) (stunt arranger – 1 episode)
  – The One That Got Away (stunt arranger)

1987
Hellraiser (stunt arranger)
Tutti Frutti (TV Mini-Series) (stunt arranger – 1 episode)
  – Love Hurts (stunt arranger)
Personal Services (stunt coordinator)
Up Line (TV Movie) (stunt arranger)

1986
Whoops Apocalypse (stunts)
The Monocled Mutineer (TV Mini-Series) (stunt coordinator - 3
    episodes)
    - When the Hurly-Burly›s Done (stunt coordinator)
    - Before the Shambles (stunt coordinator)
    - The Making of a Hero (stunt coordinator)
Biggles (stunts)
Caravaggio (stunt coordinator)
Car Trouble (stunts)

1985
The Good Father (stunt arranger)
Underworld (stunt coordinator)
Travelling Man (TV Series) (stunt arranger - 4 episodes)
    - Last Lap (1985) (stunt arranger)
    - The Quiet Chapter (1985) (stunt arranger)
    - Moving On (1984) (stunt arranger)
    -   Grasser (1984) (stunt arranger)
In Sickness and in Health (TV Series) (stunt coordinator - 1 episode)
    - Episode #1.6 (stunt coordinator)
The Adventures of Sherlock Holmes (TV Series) (stuntman - 1 episode)
    - The Greek Interpreter (stuntman)
My Beautiful Laundrette (stunt coordinator)
Yellow Pages (stunt coordinator)
Invitation to the Wedding (stunts)
Baby: Secret of the Lost Legend (stunts)
Dance with a Stranger (stunt coordinator)
Brazil (stunt performer)

1983
The Keep (stunts)
Never Say Never Again (additional stunts - uncredited)
Krull (stunts - uncredited)
Octopussy (stunt double under train: Roger Moore - uncredited) /
    (the stunt team)

1982
Tales of the Unexpected (TV Series) (stunts – 1 episode)
  – Death Can Add (stunts)

1981
For Your Eyes Only (additional stunts – uncredited)

1980
Flash Gordon (stunt double: Timothy Dalton – uncredited)
The Long Good Friday (stunts)
Star Wars: Episode V - The Empire Strikes Back (stunts – uncredited)

1979
Hanover Street (stunt double: Christopher Plummer – uncredited) /
  (stunt double: Harrison Ford – uncredited) / (stunts – uncredited)
Blake's 7 (TV Series) (stunt double – 1 episode)
  – Star One (stunt double – uncredited)

1978
Superman (stunts – uncredited)
The Word (TV Mini-Series) (stunt performer)
Force 10 from Navarone (stunt double: Harrison Ford – uncredited) /
  (stunts – uncredited)

1977
Ripping Yarns (TV Series) (stunts – 1 episode)
  – The Testing of Eric Olthwaite (stunts)
The Spy Who Loved Me (stunts – uncredited)
A Bridge Too Far (stunts – uncredited)
Star Wars: Episode IV - A New Hope (stunts – uncredited)

1976
The Eagle Has Landed (stunts – uncredited)

1970
You Can't Win 'Em All (stunts – uncredited)

1968
Where Eagles Dare (stunts - uncredited)

1967
The Dirty Dozen (stunts - uncredited)

Credit: Information courtesy of IMDb, IMDb.com. Used with
    permission.

MY MEMOIRS & ME

Are you at retirement age and looking to give something back to your children and society?

Has your life been a baby boomer rollercoaster that would make a terrific and attractive tale?

Do you want your mother or father's experiences to be immortalised for future generations?

You don't have to have been set on fire to make a great memoir! If you'd like to talk it through, with a truly personal one-to-one service, then please do visit the website:

www.mymemoirsandme.com

I look forward to hearing from you.

GRAHAM SCOTT

Jim Dowdall as Speaker and Commentator

Jim Dowdall has a great deal of experience as an after-dinner speaker (he wears a kilt for black tie). He is also an experienced commentator at military or film orientated events.

To contact Jim, please go to the Speakers Associates website at:

https://www.speakersassociates.com

or you can contact him direct at:

jim@stunt.demon.co.uk

I look forward to hearing from you.

Jim Dowdall

Printed in Great Britain
by Amazon

37905408R00097